ENVIRONMENTS

Processes and

Outcomes

Garrett Nagle
with Michael Witherick

Series Editor
Michael Witherick

Published in 2002 by:
Nelson Thornes Ltd
Delta Place
27 Bath Road
CHELTENHAM
GL53 7TH
United Kingdom

04 05 06 / 10 9 8 7 6 5 4 3 2

A catalogue record for this book is available from the British Library

ISBN 0-7487-5821-6

Page make-up and illustrations by Multiplex Techniques Ltd

Printed and bound in Great Britain by Ashford Colour Press

Acknowledgements
The authors and publishers are grateful to the following for permission to reproduce photographs and other copyright material in this book:

Longman, *Geomorphology and Hydrology* (1989), Figs 1.6, 1.7, 4.7, 5.5, 5.6; Routledge, *Fundamentals of the Physical Environment* (1987), Fig. 6.7.

Brian & Cherry Alexander – figs 4.1, 6.2, 6.3, 6.4, 6.6, 6.9, 6.10; Environmental Images – fig 6.5
Dick Roberts Photo Library – cover image
All other photos supplied by Nelson Thornes Archive.

The publishers apologise to anyone whose rights have been inadvertently overlooked and will be happy to rectify any errors or omissions.

Contents

BWd 10

1 Introduction   **4**
  A The cold environments   4
  B The formation of glacier ice   6
  C Ice sheets and glaciers   7
  D A systems view   10
  E Types of glacier   11
  F Ice ages   13

2 Glacial environments in erosional mode   **17**
  A Glaciers on the move   17
  B Moving features   20
  C Glacier surges   21
  D Glaciers at work   23
  E Landforms and landscape   26

3 Glacial environments in depositional mode   **36**
  A Moving loads   36
  B Dumping loads   38
  C Features great and small   40
  D Morainic landforms   43
  E Drumlins   46

4 Proglacial environments   **50**
  A Glacier hydrology   51
  B Meltwater erosion and transportation   55
  C Meltwater deposition   57
  D The modification of drainage   61

5 Periglacial environments   **64**
  A Climatic characteristics   64
  B Permafrost   65
  C Ground ice   68
  D Other processes   72
  E Relict landscapes   74
  F The tundra biome   75

6 Living in cold environments   **80**
  A Updated traditional activities   81
  B Mineral and energy exploitation   84
  C Settlement and transport   86
  D Tourism   90
  E Managing polar areas   93

Further reading and resources   **96**

1

Introduction

The cold environments

For most people, mention of 'cold environments' conjures up images of ice sheets, glaciers and icebergs (**1.1**). Such are often perceived as being amongst the diagnostic features of **wilderness areas**, namely those untouched and unchanging parts of the world where Nature reigns in all its majesty. Many cold environments are indeed truly dramatic in appearance, but some are by no means so. Today, the world's main ice masses exist at high latitudes, as in Antarctica and Greenland, and at high altitudes, as in the Alps and the Himalayas. But major ice sheets have also existed in the past at lower altitudes and lower latitudes, as for example in the British Isles during the Pleistocene period (**1.2**). At present, ice covers approximately 16 million km^2 of the Earth's surface, most of it being accounted for by the ice sheets of Antarctica and Greenland. The remainder mainly occurs in the form of glaciers and ice caps. Sediments created and laid down by ice sheets and glaciers account for a further 8 per cent of the Earth's land surface.

The ice-covered regions of the world have for long been of particular fascination to geographers. Perhaps it is for this reason that two chapters of this book are devoted to them. **Chapter 2** looks at the **glacial** environment from a largely erosional viewpoint. One can but marvel at the huge troughs

Figure 1.1 Spectacular Antarctic scenery

that have been gouged out of the Earth's surface by ice. In **Chapter 3** the focus shifts to the more depositional work of ice and the spreading of huge masses of glacial debris. But the term 'cold environments' applies much more widely than just to those parts of the globe that are or were covered by ice (**1.2**). Immediately beyond the ice margins lie the **proglacial** environments, where meltwater is the most powerful influence on landforms. The processes at work here and their outcomes, often referred to as **fluvioglacial**, are examined in **Chapter 4**. The proglacial zone, in its turn, gives way to the **periglacial** environments, where frost action, freeze–thaw and permafrost are the key influences on the landscape. It is at the outer margins of this zone that the cold environments finally give way to the warmer environments of the temperate world.

Figure 1.2 The distribution of ice environments, past and present, in the Northern Hemisphere

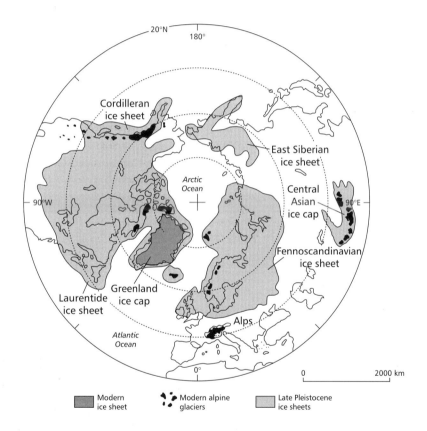

Figure **1.3** encourages us to imagine these three cold environments as forming a series of concentric zones. The underlying outward trend is one of climatic warming which, in turn, changes the nature and relative importance of landscape processes. However, we do need to make three qualifying points:

■ The boundaries between the zones are not clear-cut. Rather, there are transitional zones in which elements of 'neighbouring' environments intermingle.

Figure 1.3 The cold environments

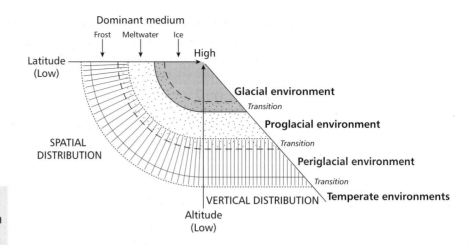

Review

1 Distinguish between **glacial**, **proglacial** and **periglacial** conditions.

2 With reference to 1.2, describe the distribution of ice sheets and glaciers during the Pleistocene.

- Climate change, both over geological time and on a short-term basis, means that all the cold environment zones expand and contract, advance and retreat (**1.3**). As one type of environment begins to 'invade' its neighbour in the concentric sequence, so the pre-existing environment undergoes modification.
- The three cold environments are not confined to the high latitudes. They also occur in mountainous areas where altitude lowers temperatures to the required levels, as for example in the Alps, Himalayas and Andes.

SECTION B

The formation of glacier ice

Snow is very much a feature of cold environments, and when that snow is converted into ice (**glacier ice** to be precise) it becomes a powerful factor moulding the landscape. Snow is frozen rain and falls initially as large hexagonal flakes. Provided that temperatures generally remain below freezing point, snow accumulates on the ground. Each new fall of snow compresses the snow beneath it, causing air to be slowly expelled. In this way, snow is gradually converted into ice. The process is known as **diagenesis**.

Snow that survives one summer is known as **firn** (a transitional state between snow and ice). It has a density of 0.4 g cm^{-3}, while **glacier ice** (the basic material of glaciers and ice sheets and which typically contains only small and isolated air bubbles) has a density of between 0.83 and 0.91 g cm^{-3}. This compares with a density of 0.92 g cm^{-3} for pure ice. Thus the density of ice and the size of ice crystals increase with time and depth. It is for this reason that true glacier ice is not encountered until a depth of at least 100 m and only comes into being after a long lapse of time. For example, in the Antarctic it takes about 1000 years to form such ice, which has a bluish or glassy green colour. Such a colour contrasts with the whiteness of firn, which is caused by the presence of air in the semi-compacted snow. The formation of glacier ice is encouraged in other ways, as for example by the seasonal melting and refreezing of surface snow. The freezing of rainwater as it hits the ice or snow surface, and the freezing of saturated air to form **rime**, may also contribute in a small way.

Review

3 Draw an annotated diagram to show the formation of glacier ice.

Ice sheets and glaciers

One thing that unites all the cold environments, besides their low temperatures, is the presence of ice – to varying degrees and in various forms. It is for this reason that the remainder of this chapter does some scene-setting about the origins of ice, its distribution, the way it works and its history.

Ice masses range from small patches to huge ice sheets such as those covering Antarctica (**1.4**). **Ice sheets** are the largest accumulations of ice, and are said to exist when ice completely and continuously covers an area of more than 50 000 km^2. At present, there are just two – Antarctica and Greenland – but during the last glacial phase (between 125 000 and 18 000 years ago) huge ice sheets also covered much of Europe (**1.2**). Today, the Antarctic ice sheet alone holds 70 per cent of the Earth's freshwater and 90 per cent of its ice. Together, the Antarctic and Greenland ice sheets account for 96 per cent of the world's ice. Of the remaining 4 per cent, two-thirds

Figure 1.4 The main forms of ice mass

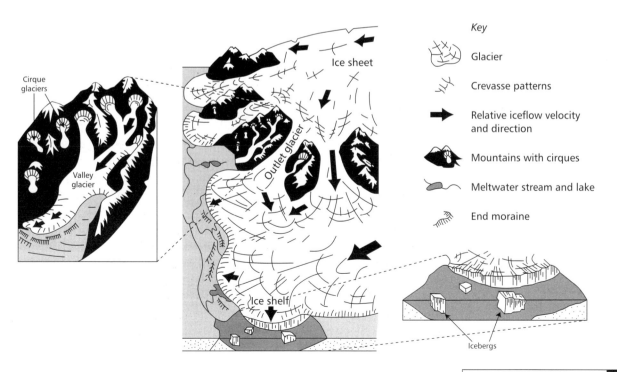

Cirque glaciers

Valley glacier

Ice sheet

Outlet glacier

Ice shelf

Icebergs

Key

Glacier

Crevasse patterns

Relative iceflow velocity and direction

Mountains with cirques

Meltwater stream and lake

End moraine

occurs in high-latitude **ice caps** (each less than 50 000 km^2 in extent), and one-third in glaciers.

Glaciers are limbs of moving ice (**1.4**). **Valley glaciers** either flow out of ice sheets and ice caps, or are independent features fed by snow and ice accumulating on mountain ranges (often referred to as **cirque** or **corrie glaciers**). In both instances, they follow the courses of pre-existing valleys or corridors of lower ground. They are often steep and may reach lengths of between 10 and 30 km. An **ice stream** is a 'fast' moving limb of an ice sheet. If ice streams become divided by mountains, they are referred to as **outlet glaciers**. An **ice shelf** is a floating mass of ice attached to the coast along one edge. The Ross ice shelf is perhaps the best known, and is of about the same extent as the state of Texas, USA. Pieces of ice shelf break off to form **icebergs**, a process known as **calving**.

Case study: The Antarctic ice sheet and sea-level change

The Antarctic ice sheet has two components: the East Antarctic ice sheet (covering an area of 10 million km^2 and in places over 4 km thick) and the West Antarctic ice sheet (2 million km^2) (**1.5**). They are separated by the Transantarctic Mountains. The former is land-based and covers ground that is currently above sea level. The latter is marine-based and is literally 'floating' on a mass of frozen sea. In the event of continuing global warming, it is the West Antarctic ice sheet that will break up and melt first. Indeed, over the last 20 000 years, all of the world's marine-based ice sheets have disappeared bar this one. In this time, the Antarctic ice front has retreated across and left exposed the Weddell and Ross Seas. If present temperature trends continue, the Larsen ice shelf in the Weddell Sea could disappear within 300 years. In 2002, 5500 km^2 of the Larsen 'B' ice shelf – an area the size of Wales – broke off.

It must be remembered that the rise in global sea level has been caused not just by the conversion of ice into water, but also by the expansion of seawater as it becomes warmer. The latter alone is currently causing sea levels to rise by about 0.6 mm each year. If the whole of the current Antarctic ice sheet melted as a result of continuing global warming, the global sea level would rise by 66 m. If the West Antarctic ice sheet alone were to melt, the rise would be restricted to about 6 m above the present level. However, even a seemingly small rise such as this would have a devastating impact on people around the world and on their settlements. Vast tracts of low-lying coastal land would be lost almost without trace beneath the sea. Perhaps there is a small crumb of comfort in the fact that the response time of ice sheets to current and any further global warming is likely to be very long. For example, it could take the West Antarctic ice sheet up to 50 000 years to respond to present rises in

Figure 1.5 The Antarctic ice sheet

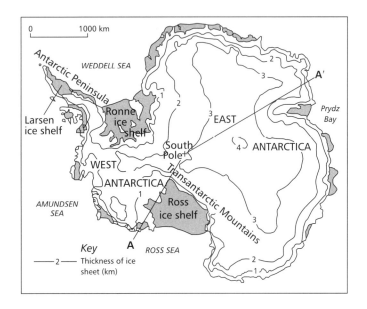

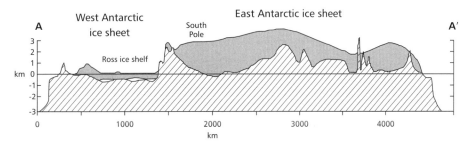

temperature. Nevertheless, small glaciers and ice shelves are likely to disappear much more quickly, but the human impact would be much less.

It has to be said that not all scientists are agreed that global warming will lead to the melting of the Earth's ice masses and to rising sea levels. There are some who argue quite the opposite, namely that global warming will increase precipitation over the currently arid polar regions. Indeed, in really cold regions, the increase might even lead to the extension of existing ice sheets and ice caps.

Review

4 Distinguish between:

■ a **glacier** and an **ice sheet**

■ an **ice stream** and an **ice shelf**.

5 Suggest reasons why the West Antarctic ice sheet may be more vulnerable to climate change than the East Antarctic ice sheet.

A systems view

Figure 1.6 The main inputs and outputs of the glacier system

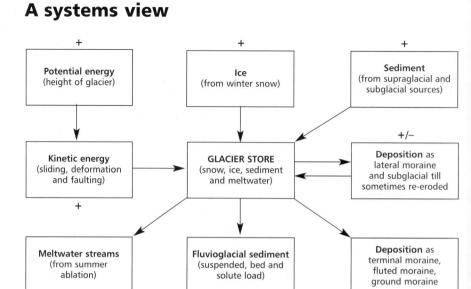

Key
+ Input
− Output

A systems view is a way of looking at how a feature, such as a glacier or ice sheet, works. All systems involve a set of **inputs**, **processes** and **outputs**. In the case of glaciers and ice sheets, the principal inputs are snow and any solid materials that are either picked up from the underlying ground or fall on to them (**1.6**). The input of snow is particularly high in what is known as the **accumulation zone** (**1.7**). Here more material is added to the ice mass than is lost. The most significant process here is diagenesis, but also to be noted is all the work done by the glacier or ice sheet as it moves. This work is perhaps more familiarly known as **erosion**, **transport** and **deposition** (see **Chapters 3** and **4**). The outputs of a glacier or ice sheet are most evident in what is known as the **ablation zone** (where more materials are lost than are gained) and include meltwater and debris (usually referred to as **moraine** and **outwash material**), as well as a great variety of landforms that are revealed as the ice front and glacier snout retreat.

Figure 1.7 Accumulation and ablation on a glacier

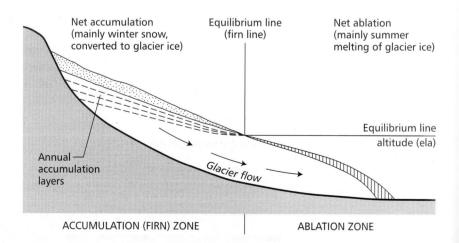

Review

6 Outline the advantages of adopting a systems view of a glacier.

7 Define the terms **accumulation** and **ablation**, and explain the significance of the **mass balance**.

8 What would you expect to be the field evidence of a glacier with a negative mass balance?

By now it should be becoming apparent that one vital aspect of the glacier or ice sheet system is the balance between accumulation and ablation, particularly over time (**1.7**). This is known as the **mass balance**. A **positive mass balance** occurs when accumulation is greater than ablation; with a **negative mass balance** the reverse situation prevails. The **equilibrium line** is the line on the surface of the glacier or ice sheet where accumulation and ablation are in balance. It is also sometimes called the **firn line**. If accumulation is greater than ablation, then the ice mass will grow and its snout or front will move forward. However, if ablation exceeds accumulation, then the volume of ice will decrease and it will shrink in extent.

The main controls in the growth or decay of a glacier or ice sheet are temperature and precipitation, working in tandem. If conditions are cold enough for precipitation to occur as snow, and if that precipitation is heavy, then it is expected that the ice mass will advance. It is this combination that explains the existence of glaciers in temperate latitudes. Here the key factor is altitude. It is this that increases precipitation and decreases temperatures to produce heavy falls of snow.

Where the climatic conditions are cold but dry, it is likely that the ice mass will remain in a 'steady state'. There will be little accumulation because of the dryness, but equally there will be little ablation or melting due to the low temperatures. This is in fact the situation that prevails in Antarctica and Greenland.

SECTION E

Types of glacier

Glaciers are frequently subdivided into two main types: **cold-based** and **warm-based**. The former are encountered largely in polar areas, whilst the latter are mainly associated with temperate regions.

Figure 1.8 Idealised temperature profiles of (a) a cold-based and (b) a warm-based glacier

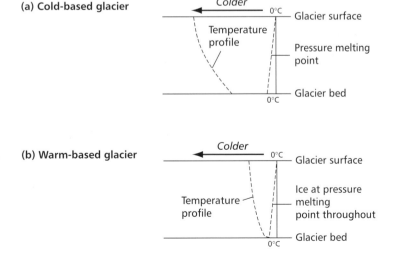

Cold-based glaciers

Largely because summer temperatures are below freezing and precipitation is low, cold-based glaciers are very slow moving. For these reasons, accumulation and ablation are limited. What little ablation that does occur does so through the medium of iceberg calving and evaporation. The typical temperature profile of a cold-based glacier is shown in **1.8a**. Since the base of the glacier is well below freezing, there is little likelihood of much movement. Indeed, very often the ice mass is literally frozen to the bedrock. Hence there is little erosion or deposition. Because little debris is carried, water bodies (such as oceans) in these areas remain very clear.

Warm-based glaciers

These are found at high altitudes in temperate locations. They are associated with high rates of accumulation and ablation. They are very active, and large volumes of ice are transferred from the accumulation zone to the ablation zone. This, together with the fact that temperatures at the glacier bed may be above freezing, means that the glacier is highly mobile and has the potential to carry out much erosion (**1.8b**). As well as wearing away the landscape, such glaciers produce much meltwater which, in turn, works on the land to create a variety of landforms, such as kames, eskers and outwash plains. Since warm-based glaciers carry much sediment, their meltwater is often milky in colour.

The mobility of glaciers and ice sheets is governed by what is known as the **pressure melting point**. This is the temperature at which ice is on the verge of melting. That critical temperature becomes lower as pressure increases. At the surface, the pressure melting point is 0°C, but within the ice mass it will be fractionally lowered by increasing pressure. Ice at the pressure melting point deforms more easily than ice below it. Most warm-based glaciers are at pressure melting point throughout the ice thickness (**1.8**), so movement is facilitated by the production of meltwater. This allows the base of the glacier literally to glide over its bed. However, in cold-based glaciers temperatures are below the pressure melting point. In the absence of meltwater, therefore, movement is only by internal flow.

Review

9 Summarise the differences between **cold-** and **warm-based glaciers** and explain the significance of the distinction.

10 Write your own definition for the term **pressure melting point**.

Ice ages

There have been many ice ages during the Earth's geological history. The earliest known one occurred some 2300 million years ago and the most recent during the course of the Quaternary period of the last 2 million years. Figure **1.9** indicates that there have been at least seven major glacial phases or ice ages. The Earth's oldest ice is found in Antarctica and some parts of it are up to 40 million years old. Drilling in the Ross Sea shows that glacier ice has been present in Antarctica for at least 36 million years. Thus the Quaternary ice age cannot be seen as discrete or isolated but, rather, it represents an intensification of glacial activity. Indeed, global temperatures fell long before the start of the Quaternary ice age, and glacial phases became much more frequent some 4–5 million years ago.

Figure 1.9 A summary of the geological time scale and major ice ages

Eon	Era	Period	Glacial phases		Age (myr)
Phanerozoic	Cenozoic	Quaternary	Antarctic	Northern Hemisphere	2
		Neogene			23
		Palaeogene			65
	Mesozoic	Cretaceous			135
		Jurassic			205
		Triassic			250
	Palaeozoic	Permian	Karoo		290
		Carboniferous			355
		Devonian	Niger		410
		Silurian	Saharan		438
		Ordovician			510
		Cambrian	Late Sinian		570
Proterozoic	Neoproterozoic		Varanger/Sturtian/ Lower Congo		1000
	Mesoproterozoic				1600
	Palaeoproterozoic		Huronian		2500
Archaean					

Despite this long history of major ice ages, most research attention focuses on the events of the Quaternary. At present, about 10 per cent of the Earth's surface is covered by ice, but as little as 18 000 years ago the figure was closer to 30 per cent (**1.2**). At this time, it is estimated that between 20 and 25 per cent of the global surface experienced periglacial conditions.

Much of the evidence of the Quaternary ice age, and indeed of climate change in general, is derived from the drilling and extraction of cores. These are mainly taken from ice masses or from seabed and lake sediments. From the former, it is possible to gather data about climate change over periods of up to 40 000 years. Ice cores contain information about changing salt, dust and isotope contents that, in turn, reflect shifts in climate. The analysis of seabed cores focuses more on their foraminifera (a form of zooplankton) and pollen grain content, each a sensitive 'barometer' of climate. More information and detail about the evidence of climate change is to be found in a companion volume in this EPICS series entitled *Climate Change and Society*.

There are a number of interrelated factors that may be the cause 'ice ages' and 'glacial phases'. They include the following:

- the 'stretch' in the Earth's orbit around the Sun
- the 'tilt' of the Earth
- the 'wobble' of the Earth's axis
- the particular distribution of land and sea
- tectonic activity.

Figure 1.10 Milankovich's ice age theory

The 95 000 year stretch
The Earth's orbit stretches from being nearly circular to an elliptical shape and back again in a cycle of about 95 000 years. During the Quaternary, the major glacial–interglacial cycle was almost 100 000 years. Glacials occur when the orbit is almost circular, and interglacials when it has a more elliptical shape.

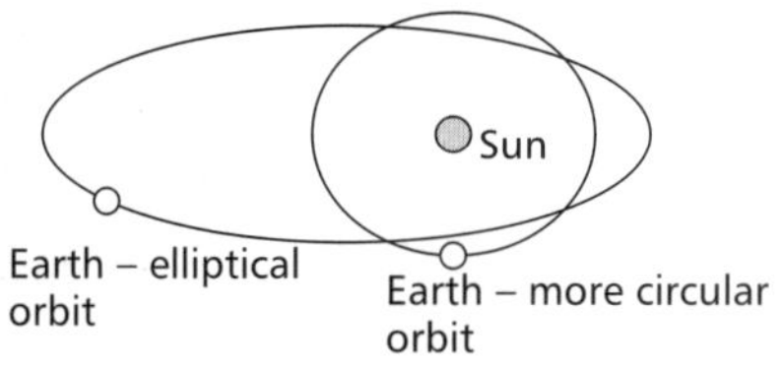

Earth – elliptical orbit
Sun
Earth – more circular orbit

The 42 000 year tilt
Although the Tropics are set at 23.5°N and 23.5°S to equate with the angle of the Earth's tilt, in reality the Earth's axis varies from its plane of orbit by between 21.5° and 24.5°. When the tilt increases, summers become hotter and winters colder, leading to conditions that favour interglacials.

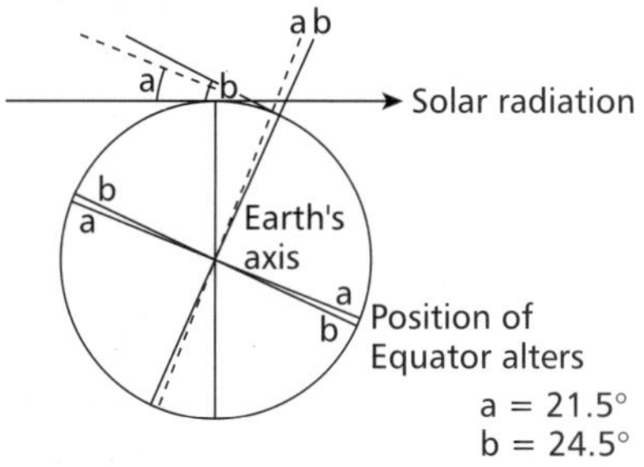

Solar radiation
Earth's axis
Position of Equator alters
a = 21.5°
b = 24.5°

The 21 000 year wobble
As the Earth slowly wobbles in space, its axis describes a circle once in every 21 000 years. At present, the orbit places the Earth closest to the Sun in the Northern Hemisphere's winter, and furthest away in summer. This tends to make winters mild and summers cool. These are ideal conditions for glacials to develop. The position was in reverse 12 000 years ago, and this has contributed to our present warm 'interglacial'.

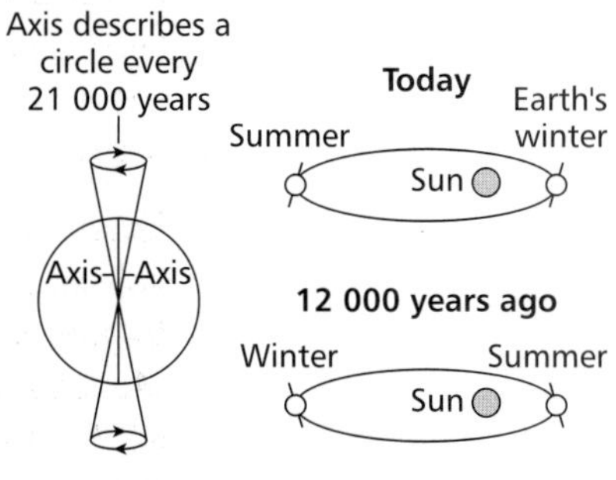

Axis describes a circle every 21 000 years
Today
Summer
Earth's winter
Sun
Axis–Axis
12 000 years ago
Winter
Summer
Sun

The first four of these factors form the basis of the theory put forward by Milankovich in the 1920s. Each of these affects the amount of insolation received at the Earth's surface, and each produces a cycle of 95 000, 42 000 and 21 000 years respectively (**1.10**). He claimed that ice ages occur when there is a particular coincidence of these three cycles, namely when:

- the Earth's orbit is circular rather than 'stretched' (elliptical)
- the 'tilt' is small
- the 'wobble' makes the Northern Hemisphere with its large land masses furthest from the Sun in summer.

Whilst there is now a considerable amount of evidence to support Milankovich's theory, it is also recognised that there are other important factors at work. For example, the distribution of land and sea changes over time. Antarctica has only existed at the South Pole for the last 300 million years. Clearly, the existence of a large land mass at this particular location greatly encourages the accumulation of snow and ice. Changes in the distribution of land and sea can also effect atmospheric and oceanic circulation. The Panama isthmus linking North and South America has only existed for 3.5 million years. Its emergence cut off an important east–west oceanic circulation, thereby strengthening the Gulf Stream and increasing the transfer of warm water high into the Northern Hemisphere. The presence of this relatively warm water in northerly latitudes has allowed more evaporation and precipitation, and thus it has favoured the growth of ice caps and glaciers.

The current **thermohaline circulation** pattern (the oceanic movement of water caused by differences in salinity and temperature) in the North Atlantic involves the movement of warm and relatively salty water northwards from the Tropics into Arctic and sub-Arctic waters. If global warming continues and there is a significant melting of ice in Greenland, Iceland and Scandinavia, the additional freshwater pouring into the ocean may cause the North Atlantic Drift to contract. Thus its warm waters might move only as far north as northern France. If this were to happen, conditions in Scandinavia and the British Isles would become much colder, thus encouraging ice masses and glaciers to grow or expand. Indeed, there is increasing evidence that circulatory changes of this nature have already occurred, namely during the last ice age – and not just once, but several times. Each time, it seems that there was some sort of **negative feedback** recovery. There are scientists today who see a causal link between the sequence of alternating glacial and interglacial phases and such changes in oceanic circulation.

Tectonic events may affect the onset of glaciation in another way. Large volcanic eruptions can throw so much ash and dust into the atmosphere as to reduce the amount of solar radiation received. The climatic impact of the Mount Pinatubo eruption in 1991 was to lower the global temperature by 0.5°C. However, an eruption of the same scale in temperate or polar latitudes would not have the same impact, since these parts of the world are areas of net energy loss.

Ice mass type	Response time (years)
Ice sheet	100 000–10 000
Large valley glacier	10 000–1000
Small valley glacier	1000–100

Figure 1.11 Ice mass response times

Review

11 Check that you understand:

  ■ the sorts of evidence used to reconstruct past climates

  ■ the nature of feedback loops, both positive and negative

  ■ the essentials of Milankovich's theory.

12 Why do different ice mass types have different response times?

Another factor that influences glacier growth and retreat is **albedo** (the reflectivity of a surface). Bright surfaces are highly reflective and so reduce the amount of incoming solar radiation that is either absorbed by the surface or trapped within the Earth's atmosphere. Thus, as ice sheets grow, so the amount of reflective surface increases and this, in turn, leads to a gradual cooling of temperature. A snowballing **positive feedback** situation is thereby created.

Finally, it needs to be pointed out that ice sheets and glaciers do not react immediately to a shift in climate (**1.11**). The response time will depend on the degree and abruptness of the change in temperature or precipitation, as well as on the size of the ice mass.

To sum up, we need to realise that the term 'cold environments' includes not just those parts of the Earth that are permanently covered by ice. Proglacial and periglacial environments beyond the ice margins are also included. However, the study of the ice-covered regions that provide the core of the cold environments requires us to recognise a number of important distinctions, as for example between ice sheets and glaciers, and between cold- and warm-based glaciers. Our general understanding of how ice masses behave is also greatly helped if we adopt a systems approach, and if we grasp the importance to that behaviour of the pressure melting point and the processes of accumulation and ablation. But overarching any study of cold environments is the fact of climate change. Climatic oscillations of different strengths, and occurring on a range of time scales, continuously and profoundly affect the extent and intensity of ice activity. Today, the evidence suggests that we are living in an interglacial period, the length and degree of which may extended by human-induced global warming.

This book seeks to take a snapshot of the world's cold environments as they are at the beginning of the third millennium AD. That snapshot may well turn out to be a portrait of environments in retreat.

Enquiry

1 Visit the British Antarctic Survey website, at http://www.antarctica.ac.uk
   Click on the press releases section and read the article 'Glacier thinning in West Antarctica'.

   ■ What is causing the thinning?
   ■ How have scientists found out that thinning is taking place?
   ■ Why is thinning a problem?
   ■ How long will it be before the Pine Island glacier disappears?

2 The Quaternary ice age is believed to have ended some 20 000–25 000 years ago. Have there been resurgences of glacial activity since then? If so:

   ■ When?   ■ Where?   ■ For how long?

Glacial environments in erosional mode

Glaciers on the move

The movement of ice is important, as it allows the glacier or ice sheet to pick up weathered debris and erode at its base and sides, as well as transport and alter the materials it carries. Large ice masses move very slowly, if at all, but small glaciers can move quite rapidly. Whilst it is generally agreed that speed profoundly affects the work that a moving ice mass does, there is a long-running debate about the effectiveness of glaciers as agents of erosion. Whilst ice is believed to be capable of eroding and transporting huge amounts of material, it is also recognised that ice, particularly if it is stagnant, is quite capable of protecting the landscape below. The mechanics of glacier erosion are complex, with both the type and the rate of movement varying according to conditional factors such as glacier size, temperature, gradient, local geology and glacial hydrology.

Case study: Glacier flow – learning the basics

In 1842, James Forbes conducted a number of experiments on the Mer de Glace glacier above Chamonix in the French Alps. He surveyed the movement of placers positioned in a line across the glacier over the whole of the summer. His observations suggested that glacier movement:

- is slow and regular
- is fastest in the middle
- declines from the surface to the base
- varies with the weather and the seasons.

He also suggested that some glaciers were frozen to their bases, whilst others were able to slide over them. Although his fieldwork methods and equipment may have been somewhat crude by today's standards, his results have survived the test of time.

The velocity of a glacier's flow is controlled by:

- the gradient of the rock floor
- the thickness of ice and its impact on the pressure melting point
- the internal temperatures of the ice.

Velocities tend to be greatest where the gradient is steep and there are large amounts of meltwater, particularly at the glacier's base.

Ice has considerable rigidity and strength. Under steady pressure, it behaves very much as a plastic or viscous body and literally flows; but under sudden compression or tension, it breaks or shears apart. In a typical glacier, then, two zones of movement may be seen:

- an upper zone of fracturing (up to 60 m deep), where the ice is brittle and breaks under sudden changes in tension to form crevasses
- a lower zone of flow, where more steady pressure and lubricating meltwater allow it to move as a viscous body.

Figure 2.1 The main types of ice flow

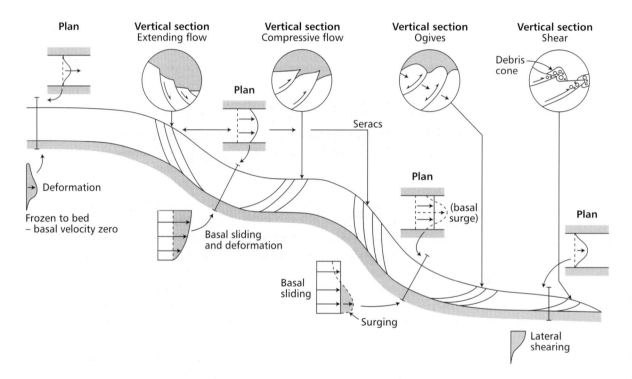

Types of flow

The mechanisms of ice movement are very complex and as yet are not fully understood. Nevertheless, a number of different types of flow have been identified in the transfer of ice from the accumulation zone, through the ablation zone and so to the ice margin (**2.1**):

- **Deformation** relates to the fact that there are different rates of movement within a moving ice mass. The sides and base of the ice move more slowly than the ice in the middle. This is the result of friction between the ice and the valley sides and bottom. This type of flow is relatively more important as a component of total glacier flow in cold-based glaciers.

- **Extending flow** occurs where the gradient of the bedrock increases; the ice accelerates and as a consequence becomes thinner.
- **Compressive flow** results from a reduction in gradient, which causes the ice to slow down and thicken.
- **Basal sliding** occurs when meltwater forms between the base of the glacier and the bedrock. This water acts as a lubricant at the interface and encourages the sliding process.
- **Regelation** is essentially an alternation of melting and refreezing that typically occurs where basal ice at pressure melting point is forced against a rock obstacle. This releases meltwater that quickly freezes again on the sole of the glacier beyond the obstacle; that is, where the pressure melting point is reduced.
- **Surging** occurs where a steepening of gradient causes a mass of ice that is already unstable to suddenly move forward (see **Section C**).
- **Lateral shearing** seems to be associated with the splaying out of ice at the glacier snout.

Case study: Subglacial deformation in an Icelandic glacier

It is difficult to study what is happening at the base of a glacier, but it has been done. In the 1980s, Boulton and Hindmarsh dug a number of tunnels in Iceland's Breidamerkurjökull glacier and through them inserted a number of cylinders into the subglacial ice. Over a period of five days, they monitored the glacier's behaviour. Analysis of the sediment at the base of the glacier showed that the upper layer of that sediment had been considerably deformed. It was calculated that up to 90 per cent of the glacier's movement was due to this subglacial deformation.

Review

1 Suggest reasons for the following:

- the importance of ice temperature to the velocity of ice movement

- the link between **regelation** and **basal slipping**

- differential flow within a glacier.

The speed of glacier movement is generally in the range of 3–300 m yr^{-1}, although where the floor is steep it may reach 1000–2000 m yr^{-1}. The most important factors determining speed of movement, besides gradient, are accumulation and ablation. High rates of accumulation and ablation mean a high throughput of ice in the glacier system. This in turn can result in relatively fast movement. Conversely, low accumulation and low ablation mean low throughput and slow movement. Movement is also greatest at the point of equilibrium: since this is where the largest quantity of ice is passing, the greatest amount of energy is available (see **1.7** on page 10).

Moving features

The movement of ice, particularly the mix of different types of flow, creates a number of distinctive features both within it and on its surface.

Crevasses

Figure 2.2 Types of crevasse

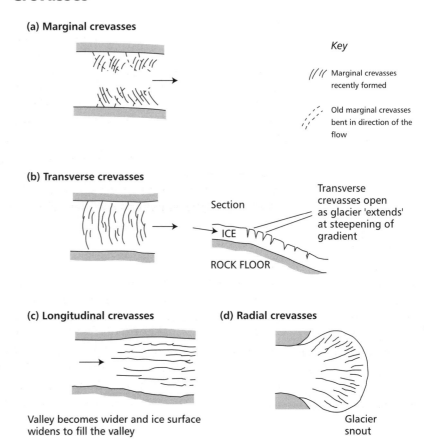

(a) Marginal crevasses

Key

/// Marginal crevasses recently formed

/ / / Old marginal crevasses bent in direction of the flow

(b) Transverse crevasses

Section

ICE

ROCK FLOOR

Transverse crevasses open as glacier 'extends' at steepening of gradient

(c) Longitudinal crevasses

Valley becomes wider and ice surface widens to fill the valley

(d) Radial crevasses

Glacier snout

Most forms of ice flow create tensions within the moving ice. If the ice lacks sufficient plasticity, various forms of fracturing or shearing may occur (**2.1**). The term **crevasse** is used to describe any deep fissure at the surface of the glacier or ice sheet. Crevasses may run in different directions relative to that of the ice movement (**2.2**):

- **marginal crevasses** are created by friction between the ice and the valley side, and are oriented roughly at 45° to the glacier edge
- **transverse crevasses** run across a glacier and are related to a steepening of gradient or a curving of the valley
- **longitudinal crevasses** run along the glacier and are created by either a local widening of the valley or a thinning of the ice
- **radial crevasses** occur near ice margins where ice has rotated and splays out – presumably they are linked to lateral shearing (**2.1**).

Seracs are pinnacles of ice formed where crevasses converge, usually at a point (an **ice falls**) where there is a marked steepening of gradient. A **bergschrund** is a gaping crack, more apparent in summer, seen around the head of an ice field (see **2.6** on page 27). It indicates an area where the ice mass is drawing away from the sides of the solid rock basin that is holding it.

Ogives

These are either cracks or, more commonly, alternating bands of light and dark ice, arranged in curves bending downstream to given an arch-like appearance in plan view (**2.1**). The bands of light-coloured ice contain more air and represent winter snow (when the rates of melting and refreezing are low). In summer, these light bands reflect heat and so do not melt very much. The darker bands are virtually air free and represent summer snow. Because of their colour, they absorb heat and so melt, taking the form of troughs on the glacier surface. These summer ogives are also darker because they contain dust blown on to the ice. The bending of the ogives is due to the faster movement in the middle of the glacier. The different properties of the winter and summer ogives creates a wave-like surface on the glacier.

Review

2 Explain the conditions giving rise to:

■ crevasses

■ bergschrunds

■ ogives.

Streams

Differential flow and compression within moving ice can also build up long, wave-like ridges of ice. Small pools, and even lakes, can accumulate in the intervening troughs: the meltwater flowing out from these troughs can erode quite deep channels in the ice surface. These **superglacial streams** will continue to flow over ice until a crevasse is reached. The stream will cascade down the crevasse and so erode a kind of sink hole known as a **moulin**. The stream may then flow within the ice as an **englacial stream** and then down to the rock floor as **subglacial stream**.

SECTION C

Glacier surges

These are short periods (less than a few months) of rapid glacier movement between long periods of relative inactivity (**2.1**). It is estimated that less than 5 per cent of all glaciers surge. Such behaviour is confined to certain regions. The characteristics of a surging glacier include:

■ a huge increase in velocity (up to 100 times the normal rate) owing to sudden additions of meltwater at the base of the glacier or a sudden change in gradient

■ surfaces pitted with crevasses due to the rapid movement of the glacier

■ large transfers of ice from the upper reservoir to the lower destination zone during the short period of surging

- a rapidly changing snout as the glacier moves into less constrained lowland regions
- the release of large volumes of meltwater.

One explanation of glacier surging is provided by the **rigid bed theory**. During quiet periods, subglacial meltwater emerges from the glacier through a single tunnel or portal. Immediately before the surge, for some unknown reason, the portal becomes blocked. The meltwater pressure increases, and as it does so, friction at the glacier bed is reduced and basal sliding suddenly increases. As the glacier becomes separated from the bedrock, a series of tunnels develops. These tunnels allow meltwater to move rapidly down through the glacier, thereby reinforcing the surge. Once the meltwater has passed through, and carried the glacier forward, the surge loses momentum and is over.

An alternative explanation hinges on the idea that the glacier may rest on a bed of soft material that is easily deformed. Permeable material can easily change to slurry if there is any increase in meltwater pressure. Thus it is thought that the glacier is able to surge over this saturated sediment.

Finally, we need to note that when ablation exceeds accumulation, and there is significant melting, ice fronts and glacier snouts retreat. But remember that even in retreat, the essential motion of the glacier or ice sheet remains forwards and downslope. As with ice movement, so rates of retreat can vary enormously (**2.3**). Rates can be as high as 20–70 m yr^{-1} in alpine glaciers. After the Pleistocene ice age, the North American, Scandinavian and British ice sheets thinned at a rate of between 0.3 and 0.5 m yr^{-1} and retreated at a rate of between 0.2 and 0.4 m yr^{-1}.

Figure 2.3 Mean rates of recent glacier retreat in selected regions

Region	Period	Mean rate of retreat (m yr^{-1})
Svalbard (Spitzbergen)	1906–1990	51.7
Iceland	1850–1965	12.2
Norway	1850–1988	28.7
Alps	1874–1980	15.6
Rocky Mountains	1890–1974	15.2
Irian Jaya	1936–1990	25.9
Kenya	1893–1987	4.8
New Zealand	1894–1990	25.9

A surging glacier was discovered on Disko Island, West Greenland, in July 1999. Within a period of four years, it was found to have advanced more than 10 km down a valley. The glacier began its surge in the autumn of 1995. In only 8 months, the glacier advanced about 8 km, and at times more than 30 m a day. The width of the glacier is approximately 1 km and it is locally more than 350 m thick. In front of the almost vertical 50–70 m glacier front, frozen fluvioglacial sediments have been pushed up to form a terminal moraine more than 30 m high. Immense water masses (estimated to about 100–150 m^3), heavily laden with sediments and huge blocks of ice, were observed pouring out of the main subglacial drainage outlet. The river plain beyond the glacier front is now up to 1.5 km wide and 12 km long and is coloured by recently deposited reddish-brown sediments. In front of the delta, sediment plumes can be followed several kilometres down the fjord.

Review

3 What is a **glacial surge** and what causes it?

4 Write a brief analytical account based on the information in **2.2**.

SECTION D

Glaciers at work

Erosion refers to the wearing away of the landscape by a moving agent. Unlike rivers, glaciers have the ability to carry huge amounts and lumps of material. For example, the Madison Boulder in New Hampshire is a **glacial erratic** – a rock transported from its source to an area of differing rock type – and is estimated to weigh over 4660 tonnes! A glacier's load comes from materials falling on to the glacier as a result of mass movements and weathering, as well as from erosion by the glacier itself of the rock surfaces containing it. This load in turn helps the glacier to erode. Although glacial erosion is commonly associated with mountain areas, glacially eroded lowlands are in fact more extensive, if less spectacular. Much of our current knowledge of glacial erosion is based not so much on direct observation of the process itself as on assumptions derived from the study of resulting landforms.

Glacial erosion consists of a number of different actions:

- **Abrasion** is often referred to as the 'sandpaper effect'. It is the erosion of the bedrock by material carried by the glacier (just like abrasion in a river). The coarser material will scrape, scratch and groove the rock, leaving striations and chatter marks; the finer material will smooth and 'polish' the rock. As ice movement continues, the glacier load will itself be worn down to form a fine rock flour.
- **Plucking** (sometimes known as **quarrying**) is the ripping out of material from the bedrock. The more fractured and broken the bedrock is, the more effective plucking becomes. This occurs mainly at the base of the glacier, but also at the sides. Plucking involves

downward pressure caused by the weight of the ice and then downhill drag as the ice moves, slowly enough for meltwater to freeze on to obstacles. Plucking is very marked in well-jointed rocks and on rocks that have been weakened by freeze–thaw weathering. Once the material has been prised out of the bedrock, it can be used for abrasion.

- **Freeze–thaw action** is an alternation that is the main cause of rock fracturing (and is recognised by some as a separate erosion process). Meltwater entering the pores and cracks of rocks expands on refreezing and gradually prises the rock apart.

Strictly speaking, freeze–thaw is not a glacial process, but is an essential component of the glacial erosion system.

Glaciers erode because they are mobile and they contain material at their base and sides. It is this material that acts as 'scraping tools', cutting away the solid rock constraining the moving ice. The coarser, more angular and harder the load is, and the faster the movement, the greater is the amount of erosion. Cold-based glaciers are far less erosive than warm-based glaciers. The amount and rate of glacial erosion also depends on the local geology. Well-fractured, jointed bedrock is easily plucked, as for example in

Figure 2.4 Factors that affect glacial abrasion

Relative hardness of particles and bedrock	Ice thickness	Basal water pressure
The most effective abrasion occurs when hard rock particles at the glacier base pass over a soft bedrock. If the debris particles are soft compared with the bedrock, the former are abraded and little bedrock abrasion is accomplished.	The greater the thickness of overlying ice, the greater is the vertical pressure exerted on particles of rock at the glacier bed and the more effective is abrasion. This is the case up to the point at which friction between particles becomes so high that movement is significantly retarded and abrasion decreases.	The presence of water at the glacier base, especially when at high pressure, can reduce the pressure on particles there and therefore abrasion rates by buoying up the glacier. However, sliding velocities may tend to increase because of reduced friction.

Presence of debris in basal ice		Sliding of basal ice
Pure ice is unable to abrade solid rock. The rate of abrasion will increase with debris concentration up to the point at which effective basal sliding is retarded.	**GLACIAL ABRASION**	Ice frozen to bedrock cannot erode unless it contains rock debris. The faster the rate of basal sliding, the more debris passes a given point per unit time and the faster the rate of abrasion.

Debris particle size and shape	Efficient removal of fine debris	Movement of debris towards glacier base
Since particles embedded in ice exert a downward pressure proportional to their weight, large blocks abrade more effectively than small particles. Moreover, angular debris is a more efficient agent of abrasion than rounded particles.	To sustain high rates of abrasion, fine particles need to be removed from the rock–ice interface, since they abrade less effectively than larger particles (assuming that the latter are being continually supplied from above). Meltwater seems to be the main medium for the removal of fine debris.	Unless particles at the base of the glacier are constantly renewed, they become polished and less effective abrasive agents. Thinning of basal ice by melting or divergent flow around obstacles brings fresh particles down to the rock–ice interface and increases abrasion.

the case of the Carboniferous Limestone of the Burren in County Clare, Ireland. A soft bedrock is also clearly more vulnerable to abrasion. Figure **2.4** summarises the various factors that affect glacial abrasion.

Case study: Measuring glacial erosion

There is still little accurate information about rates of glacial erosion. Data are extremely difficult to acquire. What follows are some of the findings achieved by geomorphologists.

In 1968, Clifford Embleton and Cuchlaine A. M. King suggested that the mean annual erosion rate for active glaciers was between 1000 and 5000 m^3. These figures compare with rates of fluvial erosion of 50 m^3 for the Mississippi River, 230 m^3 for the Colorado River above the Grand Canyon and 1000 m^3 for the Hwang Ho River. In 1984, R. J. Small observed moraines on the margins of the Tsidjiore Nouve glacier in Switzerland over a 5-year period. It was calculated that a supply of between 8728 and 11 230 tonnes of material per year was required to maintain the moraines.

Abrasion may be observed by digging tunnels through a glacier to gain access to basal cavities. Some of the best results have been provided by Geoffrey Boulton, in his 1974 work on the Breidamerkurjökull glacier in Iceland. He monitored the movement of a basalt fragment over a large **roche moutonee** (see page 31) 20 m below the surface. The basalt was removed and examined. It had been in contact with the glacier bed in three places. The basalt was scored by striations that totalled 3 m in length and varied between 1 and 3 mm in depth. The study concluded that the depth of the striations was related to the degree of abrasive activity.

Work in the Sognefjord area of Norway has revealed that during the last ice age glaciers here lowered the land surface by an average of 610 m over a period of 600 000 years.

Review

5 Distinguish between **abrasion** and **plucking**.

6 Argue the case for and against classifying freeze–thaw as a glacial process.

7 Attempt to rank the factors in **2.4** according to their importance. Justify your ranking.

Landforms and landscape

Large-scale features formed by glacial erosion include cirques, glacial troughs (U-shaped valleys), hanging valleys and fjords, while small-scale features include roche moutonees, erratics and striations (scratches on rock). Many erosional features, particularly those in lowland areas, have been protected and hidden by later glacial and fluvioglacial deposits laid down on top of them. Others, particularly those exposed by retreating ice sheets and glaciers, have subsequently been modified by later non-glacial processes.

Fore-deepening

The landscape under an ice sheet or ice cap may become fore-deepened. This means that the land beneath the centre of the ice mass becomes depressed by the sheer weight of the ice. The depression may also be accentuated by the fact that erosion tends to be greatest where the ice is thickest.

Case study: The fore-deepening of Greenland

Ice caps are formed as snow piles up over millennia in an area where it is never allowed to melt. It is slowly compressed, from bottom to top, into ice. When the weight of the ice becomes so great that the underlying land cannot support it, the land beneath the centre compresses and the ice around the edges begins to flow downward in glaciers, which may reach the sea and form icebergs.

Figure 2.5 The fore-deepening of Greenland

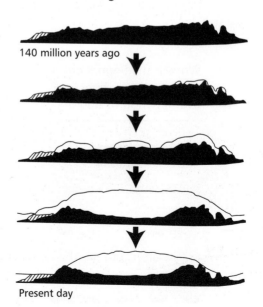

140 million years ago

Present day

Three million years ago, during the Pleistocene, a huge ice sheet developed on Greenland. Today, it measures 2500 km from north to south, 1000 km from east to west and is up to 3 km thick! The great weight of this huge ice mass has caused Greenland's surface to sink to over 3000 m below sea level (**2.5**). Without this burden, the land mass would resemble an immense bowl. In fact, there is so much water bound up in the Greenland ice sheet that if it were to melt, the global sea level would rise by at least 6 m.

Cirques

A **cirque** (or **corrie**, as it is sometimes called) is an armchair-shaped hollow surrounded by knife-edged ridges called **arêtes** (**2.6**). Cirques, along with U-shaped valleys, are among the most characteristic features of glaciated highlands. They vary in size and shape, from a few hundred metres to over 15 km wide (Walcott Cirque in Victoria Land, Antarctica, has a headwall of 3 km). Nevertheless, the length-to-height ratio – that is, from the lip to the top of the headwall – ranges from 2.8 : 1 to 3.2 : 1. For example, the ratio of the Western Cwm of Everest is 3.2 : 1, whereas that of Blea Water Corrie in the English Lake District is 2.8 : 1. Cirques are heavily influenced by the joint pattern of rocks. The rocks need to be hard enough to resist complete destruction, but weak enough to be heavily weathered and eroded. Backwalls behind cirques require destructible, near-vertical joints.

The formation of cirques is complex and a number of different processes are likely to be involved (**2.6**). In the British Isles, cirques have developed best on slopes facing between north and east. Here insolation is lowest, and this has allowed the rapid accumulation of snow. The most common theory of cirque formation is that a shallow, pre-glacial hollow is the original site of snow accumulation. The hollow is enlarged by freeze–thaw weathering at the edge of the snowpatch. This is part of a complex process known as **nivation** (see **Chapter 5**, page 73), which also involves solifluction, transport by running water and possibly chemical weathering beneath and at the edges of the snowpatch. Continuing nivation enlarges the hollow and so **firn** proper can form. As the basin is enlarged so more ice can accumulate.

Figure 2.6 The formation of a cirque

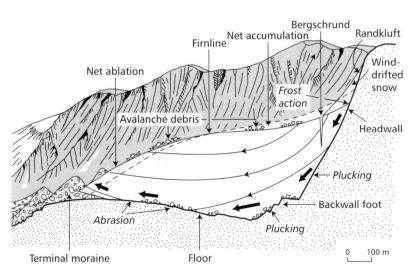

Review

8 Explain why aspect is an important factor in cirque formation.

9 Check that you understand:

■ the processes of **nivation** and **headwall recession**

■ the difference between a **bergschrund** and a **randkluft**

■ the nature of **firn**.

10 Suggest reasons why there are so few pyramidal peaks in the British Isles.

At a critical depth and weight of ice, the ice begins to move out of the hollow by extrusion flow in a rotational manner (**2.6**). This rotational movement helps the ice to erode the hollow further by plucking and abrasion, and so the somewhat semi-circular form of the cirque is gradually created. Meanwhile meltwater, especially that which makes its way down the bergschrund and **randkluft** (a gap between the rock headwall and the cirque ice, caused when heat from the rock melts the ice), helps in continuing cirque growth. As the meltwater trickles down into the cirque, it becomes the agent of freeze–thaw weathering causing the rock wall at the back of the cirque to retreat (referred to as **headwall recession**) and remain steep. Once in the basin, the meltwater also helps prepare the underlying rock for erosion by the moving ice.

When the ice finally disappears, an armchair-shaped hollow remains. It often contains a small lake dammed back by the cirque lip left as a result of the rotational movement of the ice and the deposition of moraine. Many British cirques were originally formed during the early glacial phases and subsequently modified by nivation in the later, less severe, glacial times.

If several cirques develop in close proximity to each other, there is a likelihood that headwall recession will erode the space between them until it is no more than a narrow, steep-sided ridge, known as an **arête** (**2.7**). If three or more cirques coalesce in this way, a **pyramidal peak** or **horn** will be defined between them, its shape sharpened by the processes of frost and freeze–thaw weathering. Sometimes looking somewhat similar, but with rather different origins, are the rock outcrops that protrude through ice sheets, known as **nunataks**.

Glacial troughs

Glacial troughs are characterised by steep sides and a relatively flat floor (**2.7**). Upstream, these troughs are typically defined abruptly by a steep wall known as the **trough end**. Above this, there may well be the cirques that supply the valley glacier with its ice. The troughs are usually described as being U-shaped, but few are actually of that shape; most are parabolic. They clearly result from the channelling of ice through valleys.

Glacial troughs are the outcome of a number of processes and sequences of changing conditions. Before the actual onset of glaciation and ahead of ice accumulation, active freeze–thaw weathering under periglacial conditions will weaken the floor and sides of the pre-existing valley, so preparing it for rapid erosion. Once the valley has become occupied by moving ice:

■ its course will tend to be straightened
■ its floor will be flattened
■ its sides will be steepened and spurs truncated
■ steps and basins will be created where weaker rocks are literally scooped out.

Figure 2.7 The glacial trough and its associated erosional features

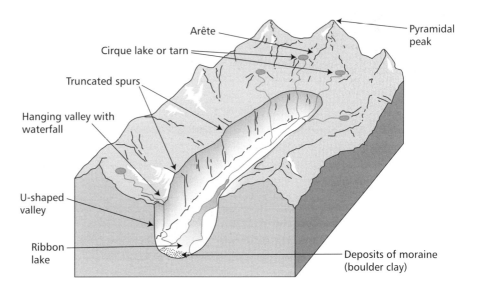

Review

11 Explain why relatively few glacial troughs are truly U-shaped.

During interglacial phases, and with the return of periglacial conditions, there will be further weathering of those rock surfaces previously stripped of their weathered material by the passing ice. The present form of most glacial troughs greatly depends on the nature of the geomorphological activity (such as weathering, mass movement, fluvial erosion and deposition, and so on) that has taken place since the last glaciation. For example, frost shattering will have produced the screes that now cover the sides of the troughs. Moraines will now lie dumped irregularly on the trough floor, here and there damming back meltwater to form more ribbon lakes and being widely reworked by contemporary river processes.

Hanging valleys

In temperate and tropical valleys, most tributary streams cut downwards to meet the level of the main river at the point of confluence. This is not the case with glaciated valleys. Tributary glaciers usually do not have the weight or the power to keep pace with the main glacier as it lowers its trough floor. Tributary ice entering the main valley may well simply slide down on to the top of the glacier. When the ice eventually melts and disappears, the tributary valleys are often left perched high above the main valley as **hanging valleys**. Waterfalls frequently draw our attention to the existence of such valleys. In Yosemite National Park, California, the Ribbon and the Bridal Veil Falls both involve drops of several hundred metres down the side of the main valley.

Fjords

Fjords are glacial troughs that are wholly or partly below sea level, their 'drowning' being the outcome of overdeepening and the general post-glacial rise in sea level (**2.8**). Up to one quarter of fjords have active glaciers. Fjords are more likely to be U-shaped than land-based glacial troughs. This is because most fjords retain their clean ice-eroded sides, whilst land-based troughs are often covered with post-glacial deposits of scree and other weathered materials.

Figure 2.8 The formation of a fjord

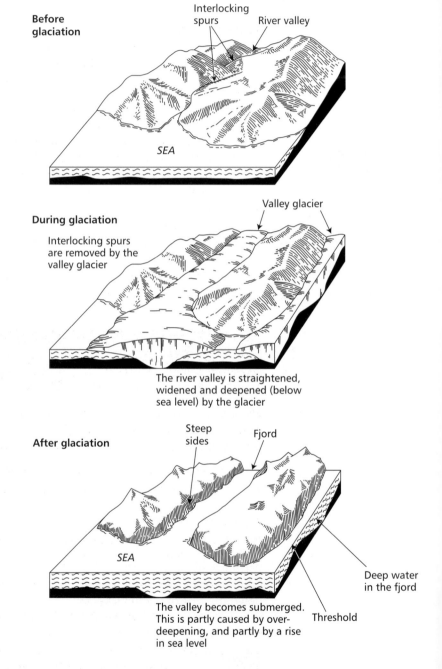

Before glaciation

Interlocking spurs
River valley
SEA

During glaciation

Interlocking spurs are removed by the valley glacier

Valley glacier

The river valley is straightened, widened and deepened (below sea level) by the glacier

After glaciation

Steep sides
Fjord

SEA

Deep water in the fjord

The valley becomes submerged. This is partly caused by over-deepening, and partly by a rise in sea level

Threshold

Review

12 With reference to either hanging valleys or fjords, comment on the claim that variations in rates of glacial erosion provide the key to understanding their origins.

The long profiles of many fjords show a considerable deepening near the head and then a very gentle slope towards the seaward end (**2.8**). The mouth itself is often marked by a sill or threshold of rock or moraine. This is thought to reflect the reduction in the glacier's erosive power as its approaches the sea. The Sognefjord in Norway has a maximum water depth of over 1300 m, but at the mouth this is only 200 m. In the Scottish lochs of Morar and Maree, the sills have been raised above sea level by isostatic uplift that has followed deglaciation.

Minor features

There are a number of smaller landscape features associated with glacial erosion. These include the following:

- **Rock steps** occur on the floors of glaciated valleys. They are related to joints, faults and other geological weaknesses that have been accentuated by the valley glacier.
- **Domes and whalebacks** are areas of bare rock, abraded and streamlined by passing ice, and in the case of the former then subjected to **exfoliation**, a form of weathering as a result of which outer layers of rock peel off. The latter are sometimes known as **rock drumlins**.
- **Roche moutonees** are huge masses of ice-moulded rock, usually projecting above the general level of the trough floor. The upflow side has been smoothed by glacial abrasion, whilst the downflow side is jagged and bears the scars of glacial plucking. Because of these twin features, roche moutonees are useful landforms in helping us to work out former patterns of ice movement, particularly beneath ice sheets.

Review

13 Can you think of any other small-scale features that are created by glacial erosion?

Case study: Glacial features in Snowdonia

Snowdonia is an excellent example of a glaciated area. Within its small extent can be found a range of glacial and fluvioglacial features. The landscape has been heavily influenced by two great events:

- tectonic uplift and deformation 435 million years ago
- the Pleistocene glaciations of the past 1.6 million years.

The tectonic period created the hard, resistant igneous and metamorphic rocks that now characterise the area, whilst the glacial period largely moulded the landscape into its present form.

At the peak of glaciation, some 18 000 years ago, the equilibrium line altitude (the lower limit of accumulation and hence cirque formation) was just 300 m, and an ice sheet of over 2000 km^2 covered North Wales. Four thousand years later, the ice sheet was in marked decline, but the corrie glaciers remained active for much longer, feeding the valley glaciers that radiated out beyond the margins of the retreating ice sheet.

The processes and features associated with the glaciation of Snowdonia can be conveniently divided into four main zones (**2.9**):

Figure 2.9 The glaciation of Snowdonia

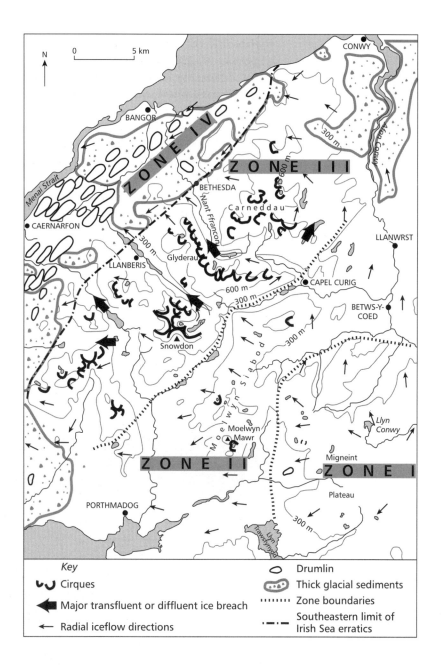

- **Zone I** coincides with the location of the central ice sheet. Here there was very little ice movement, and hence limited glacial action. The ice sheet buried the landscape, leaving just a small number of nunataks exposed. What remains of the area covered by the ice cap is the plateau surface with abraded rocks and shallow lakes. It contains none of the typical features of upland glaciation.
- **Zone II** is a belt of selective erosion. Away from the centre of the ice sheet, ice began to erode bedrock channels, and deposition subsequently occurred as the ice retreated. However, the evidence of erosion is dominant, particularly the **cnoc and lochan** landscape created by basal

erosion. The cnocs (hills) are roche moutonees, while the lochan (lakes) occupy eroded rock basins.

- **Zone III** is the zone at the former margins of the ice sheet, with outlet and cirque glaciers. Here the ice was 'warmer'; it moved at greater velocity and it eroded the landscape with great power. Erosional features abound. For example, there are some 15 cirques aligned along the North Glyderau upland and overlooking the Nant Ffrancon Valley (see below).
- **Zone IV** is the piedmont zone. Erosion in the mountains of Zones II and III led to a huge amount of deposition on the lowlands here, both by the glaciers themselves and also by meltwater. We will take a closer look at this zone in the next chapter.

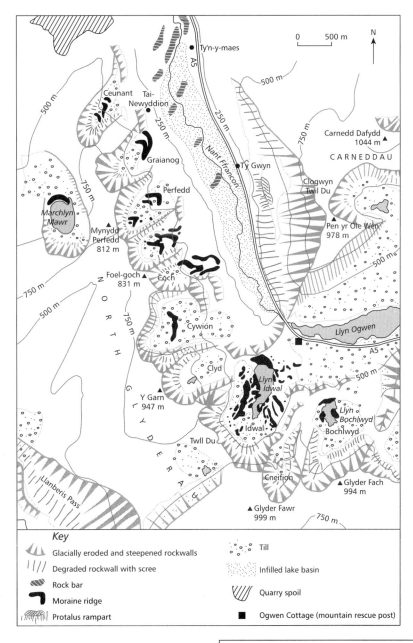

Figure 2.10 The Northern Glyderau cirques and Nant Ffrancon (Wales)

Figure 2.11 A view of Snowdonia

The Nant Ffrancon Valley shows evidence both of ice sheet and cirque glaciation. The valley, cut into the Glyderau–Carneddan massif, is an unusual glacial trough (**2.10**). True, it has very steep sides and a flat floor, but whilst seven cirques are cut into its west side, there are none on the east. All of these cirques, plus the other seven on the North Glyderau, all face between 40°E and 75°E. Insolation is the crucial factor that explains this directional consistency.

The Nant Ffrancon trough is now considered to be but a short segment of a much longer valley that once cut across the whole of the Snowdonia region. It is now regarded as an example of a transfluent trough. Outlet glaciers from the North Wales ice sheet swept through the valley, eroding and deepening it. Llanberis was formed in a similar way. There is also a second smaller trough within the valley, which has since been infilled with sediment. The trough as a whole contains many classic glacial erosional features, such roche mountonnees, truncated spurs, rock basins and striations – not forgetting the amazing concentration of cirques just mentioned.

Review

14 Explain the relationship between the four zones defined in 2.9.

15 Suggest reasons why glacial activity was limited in some parts of North Wales but very extensive in others. Use examples to support your answer.

The aim of this chapter has been to show that ice masses move, largely under the influence of gravity. They move in a variety of ways and at different speeds. When moving, ice has the potential to become a powerful erosive force. A whole series of distinctive landforms is created by the erosive modification of the pre-existing landscape. But erosion is only one outcome of moving ice. Two others – the transport and deposition of weathered material – are considered in the next chapter.

1   Study the data in **2.12**, which were derived over a period of 21 days.

		Subglacial flow (cumecs)	Total discharge (cumecs)
August	13	5	9
	14	4	12
	15	4	17
	16	5	16
	17	7	10
	18	8	10
	19	6	8
	20	5	8
	21	5	12
	22	6	13
	23	7	7
	24	5	5
	25	3	3
	26	2	2
	27	1	1
	28	1	2
	29	1	3
	30	2	4
	31	2	6
September	01	5	8
	02	4	10

Figure 2.12 Discharge data for the Gorner glacier (Switzerland)

   a Plot the data on a graph.
   b Comment on the relationships shown by the graph.
   c Suggest reasons for the relationships.

2   Visit the British Antarctic Survey website, at

http://www.antarctica.ac.uk

and research data that has been collected about ice movement and erosion.

Glacial environments in depositional mode

Moving loads

In the previous chapter, we examined how and why ice sheets and glaciers move, and how they acquire their load. We now investigate what they do with and to their load, and what happens to it when it is eventually dropped. There is no doubt that moving ice is capable of carrying enormous loads. Glaciers act like giant conveyor belts, carrying masses of material that are eventually deposited when it reaches the glacier snout. Deposition can also occur earlier at other locations within the glacier, particularly if it is retreating and where the velocity of movement is reduced. A glacier's load can be carried:

■ **subglacially** – under the glacier
■ **englacially** – within the glacier
■ **supraglacially** – on top of the glacier (**3.1**).

In all cases, most of the load is transported either by a process of pushing or because it is held within the mass of moving ice.

The load of a glacier can be highly variable in size. The material is typically unsorted and made up of angular rock fragments. The unsorted nature is due to the complex flows taking place within a glacier and to the limited impact of running water. The angularity simply reflects the status of freeze–thaw weathering as a dominant process in the areas supplying load and the lack of **attrition** (the wearing away of particles of debris by contact with other such particles) that might make those fragments rounder.

Figure 3.1 Sources of load and modes of transport

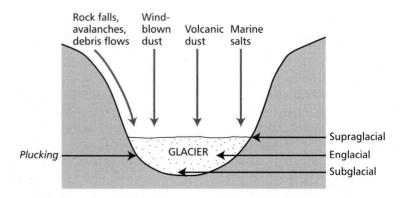

However, it has to be said that as one moves from the surface to the base of a glacier, the degree of angularity does decrease.

The material transported by ice sheets and glaciers comes from many sources (**3.1**):

- **Rockfalls** down adjacent valley slopes are a major source feeding debris on to the glacier.
- **Avalanches** similarly feed a mixture of snow, ice and rocks from the same direction.
- **Debris flows** are important in areas where there is a high level of precipitation and relatively warm temperatures. When melting snow or rain combines with scree, mud and soil, mobile flows can be created that are capable of quickly delivering large quantities of material on to the glacier conveyor belt.
- **Wind-blown dust** can be a significant source, particularly near the ice margins and glacier snouts. Here, strong winds blowing over outwash sands and gravels can pick and deliver finer particles to the surface of the glacier.
- **Volcanoes** can be a source of material in tectonically active areas such as Iceland, supplying wind-borne ash and dust.
- **Marine salts** can be an important component of a glacier's load in areas close to the sea, such as around the edge of the Antarctic ice sheet.

Figure 3.2 The story of moraine: (a) during glaciation; (b) after glaciation

(a) During glaciation

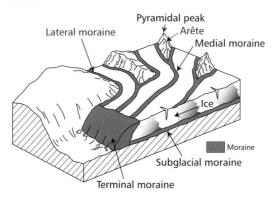

(b) After glaciation

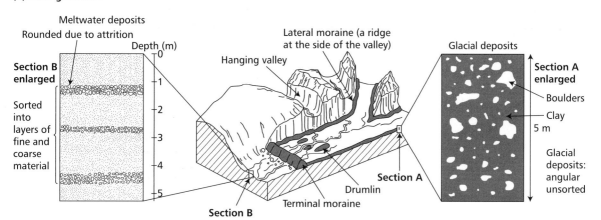

Moraine is the term that is widely used when referring to most of the material carried by a glacier (**3.2a**). It is also used in naming the specific landforms created out of this material. Rockfalls, avalanches and debris slides are the major source of supply of glacier load. Much of this material is delivered initially to the surface, where it is referred to as **supraglacial moraine**. Subsequently, it moves down crevasses, moulins and other seasonal meltwater routes into the body of the glacier. It then becomes known as **englacial moraine**. Some of this material may eventually reach the base of the glacier and become **subglacial** or **ground moraine**. But the major source of ground moraine is the weathered material that the glacier itself has plucked from the floor and sides of the pre-glacial valley.

Review

1 Check that you know the main sources of a glacier's load.

2 How might the load of a glacier differ from that of an ice cap?

3 Give reasons for the following:

- the decrease in the angularity of moraine from the surface to the base of a glacier

- the creation of lateral moraines

- some supraglacial moraine eventually becoming subglacial moraine.

SECTION B

Dumping loads

In general, glaciers drop their load either when there is some decrease in velocity or when there is **deglaciation** (melting and retreat). With the former, the deposition is only ever partial, but with the latter it can be complete. Direct deposition from a glacier, be it at the base or at the snout, involves masses of unstratified and unsorted material called **till**. This is sometimes also referred to as **boulder clay** (**3.2b**). Moraine is also deposited indirectly through the medium of meltwater, which picks up load carried by the ice before it thawed. This material is moved, often to beyond the ice limits, and eventually deposited. The whole process is known as **fluvioglaciation**. Because of water action, fluvioglacial deposits are typically sorted and stratified.

We need to remain alive to this distinction between glacial and fluvioglacial deposition. When it comes to landforms, admittedly the distinction is far from clear-cut, but in this chapter attention is focused on the former mode of deposition. The latter is considered in much more detail in **Chapter 4**. **Drift** is a collective term used to embrace both types of deposit – till and fluvioglacial (**3.3**).

Figure 3.3 The two main components of drift

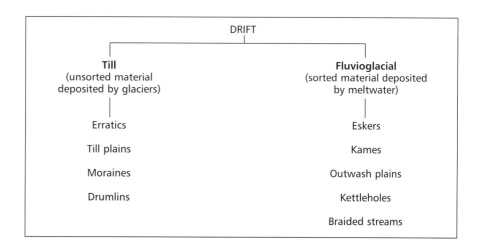

```
                              DRIFT
              ┌─────────────────┴─────────────────┐
           Till                              Fluvioglacial
     (unsorted material                (sorted material deposited
      deposited by glaciers)                 by meltwater)
              │                                   │
           Erratics                             Eskers

          Till plains                           Kames

           Moraines                        Outwash plains

           Drumlins                          Kettleholes

                                           Braided streams
```

Figure 3.4 Typical drift thicknesses in lowland areas and on continental shelves

Continent	Location	Thickness (m)
Antarctica	McMurdo Sound	702
	Prydz Bay	480
Europe	Norrland (Sweden)	7
	Denmark	50
	North Germany	58
	Mecklenburg (Germany)	470
	Heidelburg (Germany)	397
	Po Valley (Italy)	800
	North Sea	920
	East Anglia	143
	Isle of Man	175
North America	Gulf of Alaska	5000
	Fraser Delta	670
	Spokane Valley	390
	Great Lakes	232
	Illinois	12
	Central Ohio	29

Review

4 Distinguish between **glacial** and **fluvioglacial** deposits.

5 What tentative conclusions might you draw from the data in **3.4**?

At present, glacial sediments cover up to 8 per cent of the Earth's surface. In Europe, however, the figure is around 30 per cent and in North America 25 per cent. Much of this cover represents load that has been left by ice masses that have shrunk and disappeared. However, beneath the glaciers and ice sheets that survive today, it has been estimated that direct deposition of load has taken place at rates up to 6 m per 100 years. Figure **3.4** provides some information about drift thicknesses on three continents.

Features great and small

The landforms resulting from glacial deposition are neither as rugged nor as impressive as the erosional landforms – 'low' and 'smooth' are two adjectives that spring to mind. But for all that, deposition features can be as complex as anything resulting from erosion. This is due in no small part to the very nature of melting (deglaciation), in that the relatively new landforms formed beneath the passing ice are soon affected and influenced by meltwater and periglacial processes.

The morphological results of glacial deposition range from impressive landforms such as terminal moraines to almost inconspicuous features such as layers of till and erratics (**3.5**). Let us take a look at these, starting with those features that lie at the 'inconspicuous' end of the range.

Erratics are arguably the smallest expressions of glacial deposition. They are nothing more than pieces of rock. Whilst they vary enormously in size from pebbles to huge boulders, the key thing is that, geologically speaking, they are out of place. They relate to rock outcrops that occur elsewhere. They have been picked up by the moving ice, transported often over quite long distances and then dumped, usually on flat areas. The size of an erratic depends on:

Figure 3.5 A classification of glacial depositional features

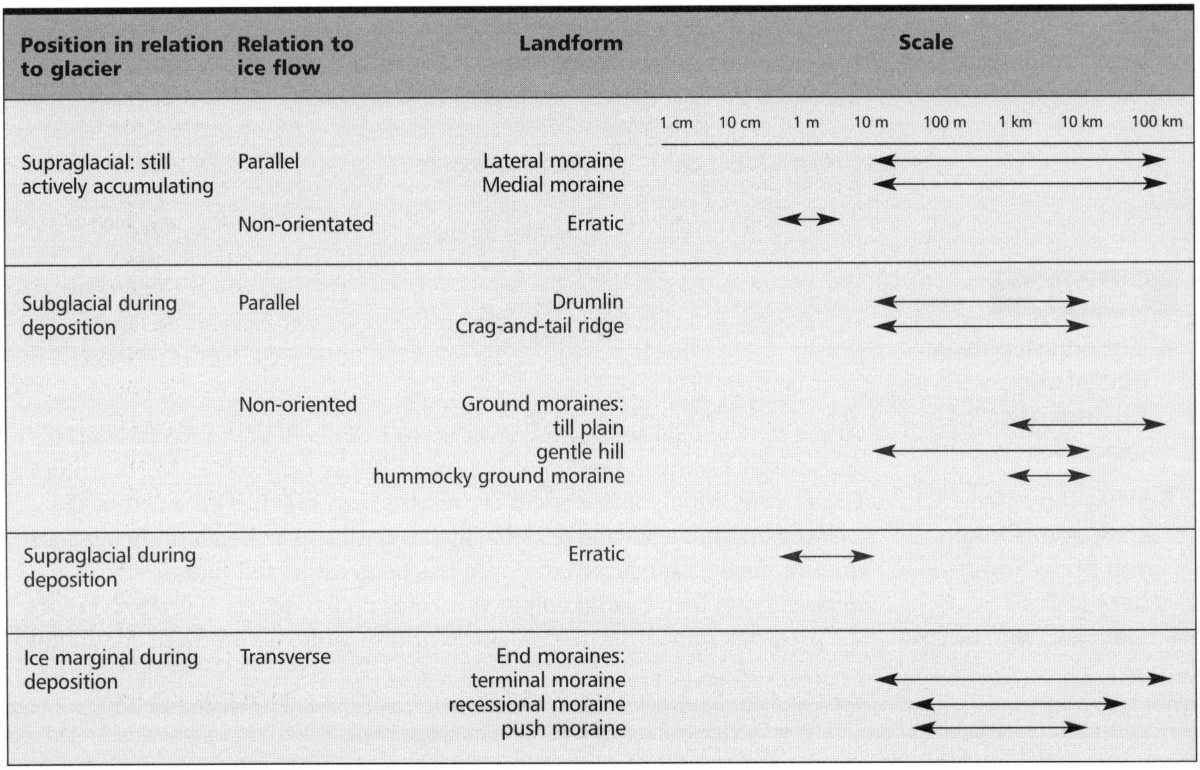

- the characteristics of its rock, such as hardness and jointing
- the length of time it was being moved by the ice
- the power of the moving ice.

Position in relation to glacier	Relation to ice flow	Landform	Scale
			1 cm　10 cm　1 m　10 m　100 m　1 km　10 km　100 km
Supraglacial: still actively accumulating	Parallel	Lateral moraine	100 m ←————————————→ 100 km
		Medial moraine	100 m ←————————————→ 100 km
	Non-orientated	Erratic	1 m ←→ 10 m
Subglacial during deposition	Parallel	Drumlin	100 m ←————————→ 10 km
		Crag-and-tail ridge	100 m ←————————→ 10 km
	Non-oriented	Ground moraines: till plain	10 km ←————→ 100 km
		gentle hill	100 m ←————————→ 10 km
		hummocky ground moraine	10 km ←→
Supraglacial during deposition		Erratic	10 cm ←———→ 1 m
Ice marginal during deposition	Transverse	End moraines: terminal moraine	1 km ←————————→ 100 km
		recessional moraine	100 m ←————————→ 10 km
		push moraine	100 m ←————————→ 10 km

The Norber Stone on the North York Moors and the Bowder Stone in Borrowdale in the Lake District are spectacular examples of glacial erratics. In other instances, erratics have been left stranded by the ice in precarious positions, and are referred to as **perched blocks**. All in all, and particularly where highly distinctive rock types are involved, erratics can provide useful information about the directions of former ice movements. This is well illustrated by erratics derived from the unusual bluish micro-granite of Ailsa Craig, a tiny island off the Ayrshire coast in Scotland. Rocks from this localised source have been found along much of the east coast of Ireland, as well as along the west coast of Lancashire and Wales and at least 250 km away (**3.6**).

Till or **boulder clay** plains are the direct result of glacial deposition. Although they may be inconspicuous as far as relief is concerned, in terms of area covered and the degree to which they modify the pre-glacial landscape, they are the most important of all glacial depositional features (**3.6**). Such plains are formed where large masses of unstratified drift smother the underlying rocks. High points of the pre-glacial surface beneath the drift may protrude through to break up the otherwise level surface. The till itself is very variable in composition, comprising finely grained sands and clays mixed together with rock of all shapes and sizes. The precise composition depends on the nature of the rocks over which the ice has moved. The size of much of the material depends very much on how far it has travelled since being picked up by the ice. In general, the further the travel, the more the material is likely to be reduced in size by general process of attrition. Compaction by the weight of overlying ice often leads to a relatively hard deposit, particularly where there is a high clay content.

Figure 3.6 Glacial deposition in the British Isles

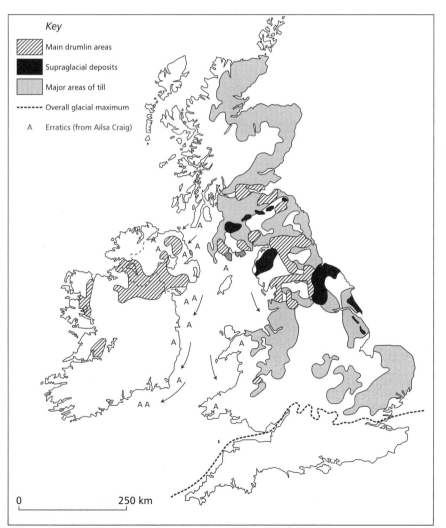

Key

- Main drumlin areas
- Supraglacial deposits
- Major areas of till
- - - - - Overall glacial maximum
- A   Erratics (from Ailsa Craig)

0   250 km

When it comes to investigating glacial till, two main categories are recognised. The **primary tills** are those that are still in their original state. On the other hand, **secondary tills** are those that have subsequently been reworked and re-deposited by ice. However, they have not been affected by meltwater. In landform terms, however, there is little to distinguish between these different types. In both cases, an investigation of the orientation of stones and pebbles within the till, using a technique known as **till fabric analysis**, can tell us much about the direction of former ice movements.

Case study: Till fabric analysis

In its simplest form, this involves measuring the orientation and dip of the long axes of a sample of 50–100 stones contained within a till. These are then plotted on a rose diagram to show the general orientation (if any) of the stones (**3.7**).

Figure 3.7 Till fabric analysis of a sample of moraine

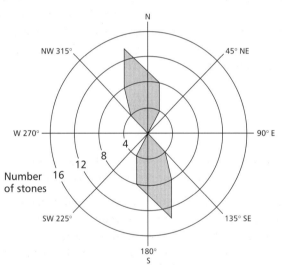

The assumption is made that the stones in ground moraines have become aligned, within the ice, parallel to the direction of flow. Furthermore, it is assumed that they retain their orientation and dip as deposition takes place. Thus till fabric analysis allows the direction of ice movement to be reconstructed, even for old tills, provided that they have not been disturbed by local slumping, freeze–thaw action or later ice advances. Such disturbance is to be suspected if the stones in a sample dip from the horizontal.

Case study: The till plain of East Anglia

One of the best examples of a till plain in the British Isles is to be found in East Anglia (**3.6**). It has a distinctly featureless surface (except in the west, where the Chalk is exposed) into which gentle valleys have been cut. The most widespread deposit here is the so-called 'chalky boulder clay' – a stony clay containing fragments of chalk and flint, together with erratics derived from rocks outside the region, such as the Jurassic rock outcrops to the north and west. The till covering is variable in depth. It commonly reaches a thickness of between 30 and 50 m, but in places it is more than 75 m deep.

The history of the East Anglian till plain is a complex one. Several different tills are now recognised as having been laid down by a number of distinct ice advances. For example, in places the chalky boulder clay overlies an earlier and weathered till deposit, known as the Norwich Brickearth. This contains a large number of erratics of Scandinavian origin and therefore clearly suggests ice movement from a rather different direction.

Review

6 Explain the importance of erratics in the study of glaciation.

7 Distinguish between **till** and **drift**.

8 Describe the distribution of major till areas as shown in **3.6**.

9 What conclusions do you draw from **3.7** about the direction of ice movement?

While sheets of till are more or less evenly spread, in detail they are gently undulating or even hummocky, with the depressions filled with lake water as on the North European Plain in Germany. The degree to which till deposition leads to the development of an entirely new physical landscape depends on a number of factors, particularly the thickness of the drift itself. Where the drift is exceptionally thick, the pre-glacial valleys may have been completely plugged, in which case an entirely new and discordant system of streams and valleys will have been etched on the surface of the plain. More commonly, however, the post-glacial drainage pattern is found to follow the lines of valleys in solid surfaces below the till.

SECTION D

Morainic landforms

Moraines are simply accumulations of glacial debris, but they create a variety of different landforms. They may be classified in several ways:

- **Position** – we saw at the end of **Section A** that position with respect to the body of the glacier allows a distinction to be made between **supraglacial**, **englacial** and **subglacial** or **ground moraine**.
- **Orientation** – relative to the direction of ice movement, this is the basis of distinguishing between **lateral**, **medial**, **terminal** and **recessional moraines**.
- **State of activity** – **active moraines** are those still in contact with moving ice, whilst **inactive moraines** have become detached from the ice that gathered them.
- **Mode of formation** – **ablation moraine** is material that has accumulated on the surface of the glacier by the gradual melting of ice. It is distinguished by its relatively coarse nature, because fine material has been washed out by meltwater. By contrast, **ground moraine** is deposited subglacially.

Perhaps the most significant of the four distinctions in terms of landforms is that based on orientation (**3.2**). Much moraine is derived from loose weathered rock that moves down valley sides and is gradually fed on to the glacier below. The combination of this load supply and the movement of the glacier creates lines of debris that gradually become part of the moving body of ice. This is **lateral moraine**. With the eventual melting or retreat of the glacier, such accumulations of moraine appear as linear embankments running along the valley sides. Good examples of lateral moraines in the British Isles are to be found at Cwm Idwal in North Wales (**3.8**). Lateral moraines of greater global renown include those along the Tasman glacier in New Zealand.

Medial moraines are formed when two glaciers meet (**3.2**). The two lateral moraines that converge subsequently flow as one in the middle of the enlarged glacier. Medial moraines are often rather superficial features, being made up of only a metre or so of coarse stony debris lying on the ice. The material is largely supraglacial. Because of this, they rarely give rise to significant landforms in post-glacial times. For example, the Kaskawash glacier in the Yukon (USA) has left a medial moraine that is 1 km wide at the point of confluence, but this quickly narrows to 60 m within a downstream distance of less than a kilometre. At a point 4 km further down, it has slimmed to only 7 m.

Terminal moraines mark the maximum advance of a glacier (**3.2**). Since they form at the snout, they are typically arc-shaped. Cape Cod in the northeastern USA is in fact a terminal moraine. Few valley glaciers today have well-defined terminal moraines that are in contact with the ice. This is because most glaciers are retreating. Terminal moraine marks the boundary between the glacial and proglacial environments. Related to this is the fact that they sometimes dam up meltwater to form marginal lakes, particularly when the ice retreat is rapid. Examples of lakes of this type are seen in front of Skeidarárjökull in Iceland.

The morphology of a terminal moraine will depend on:

- the amount of material carried by the ice
- the rate of ice movement
- the rate of ablation and thus the amount of meltwater.

The angle of the slope facing the ice (the **ice-contact slope**) is always steeper than the **meltwater slope**. The former are typically inclined between 20° and 30°; the latter between 10 and 20°. However, most terminal moraines have undergone significant modification since their formation, including a general lowering of their slopes. One of the terminal moraines of the Franz Joseph glacier in New Zealand is 430 m high. In east Denmark, the ice sheet of the Weichsel glaciation remained stationary at its maximum extent for long enough to build up morainic hills that reached to an altitude well above their present height of 173 m.

Recessional (stadial) moraines

Whilst a terminal moraine marks the maximum extent of a glacier, it needs to be understood that moraines may also be deposited by a glacier as it subsequently retreats (**3.5**). Such deposition might be expected to run at right angles to the direction of ice movement and therefore parallel to the terminal moraine. However, for such recessional moraines to become conspicuous ridges, it is vital that the ice front should remain stationary for a sufficiently long period of time. The longer the ice pauses, the greater is the deposition and therefore the larger the ridge. If the **stillstand** is long enough, the recessional moraine may in exceptional circumstances build up to a height of over 100 m. This is most likely to occur in mountain valleys, where the steep valley gradient, rapid ice flow and intense glacial

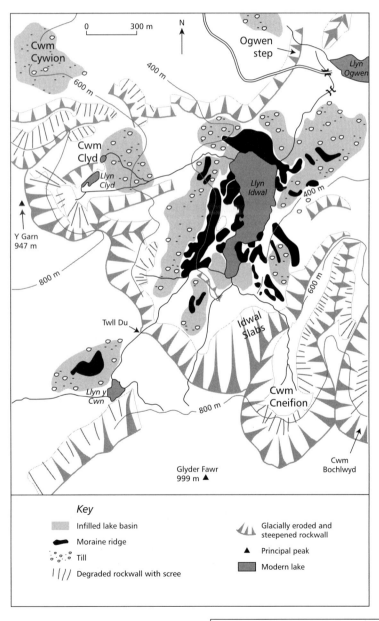

Figure 3.8 The glacial features of Cwm Idwal, North Wales

erosion deliver a huge load of morainic material to the glacier snout. Alternatively, if the ice is affected by periods of retreat separated by stillstands, a series of smaller, sub-parallel ridges will be formed.

It should be noted that terminal and recessional moraines, together with what are known as **push moraines**, are collectively referred to as **end moraines** (3.5).

It is important to remember that morainic landforms, particularly terminal and recessional moraines, are liable to modification or even destruction by meltwater issuing from the nearby ice front. The form of any recessional or terminal moraine depends on the relative roles of ice and water in their deposition and on the extent to which they have subsequently been dissected. In theory, a moraine due to deposition by ice alone will comprise a curvilinear ridge or line of low hills. Some breaks might occur to allow the passage of meltwater streams from the base of the ice. In cross-profile, however, the symmetry of the ridge may be distorted by the deposition of outwash material in the form of fans on the downstream side. Thus ice-contact and meltwater slopes typically show different profiles.

Review

10 How does a **lateral moraine** differ from a **medial moraine?**

11 Describe and explain the typical characteristics of a **terminal** or **recessional moraine**.

12 Find out what distinguishes a **push moraine**.

13 Study **3.8**, which shows some glacial features in Cwm Idwal. Describe the distribution of glacial deposition features and suggest possible reasons for the pattern.

14 Draw an annotated sketch of the Cromer Ridge based on an OS map of appropriate scale.

Case study: The Cromer Ridge (Norfolk)

The Cromer Ridge is probably the most outstanding glacial feature in East Anglia. It is in fact a terminal moraine, extending inland from the coast between Cromer and Mundesley. In places, it reaches a height of 90 m. The southern side of the ridge is less steep than the northern, which would have been in contact with the ice. The Cromer Ridge was 'pushed' into its present position by ice sheets moving from the North Sea. Before the retreat of the ice, meltwater deposits were carried over the ridge and deposited to form a gently sloping outwash plain. There is also evidence of fluvioglacial deposition on the north side of the ridge. This might be explained in two different ways. It was due either to the build-up of meltwater against the retreating ice front or, more likely, to the formation of a delta in a lake ponded between the ice and the terminal moraine ridge.

SECTION E

Drumlins

Strictly speaking, drumlins are yet another landform associated with morainic debris, but they are highly distinctive, and it is for this reason that they have a whole section devoted to them. The term **drumlin** comes from the Gaelic words *drum* (a small mound or hill) and *lin* (long). Drumlins are large mounds of glacial debris that have been streamlined into elongated small hills. They can range in size from a few metres

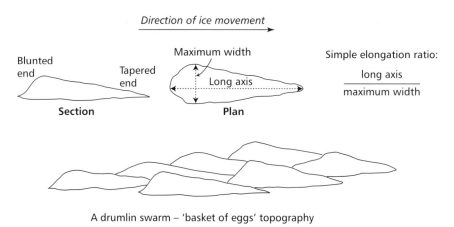

A drumlin swarm – 'basket of eggs' topography

Figure 3.9 Drumlin shape and measurement

long and high to considerable hillocks over a kilometre long and nearly 100 m high.

In plan view, they typically appear pear-shaped, with the long axis aligned with the direction of ice flow and the higher and wider end facing the direction from which the ice came. Although generally mound-like, drumlins assume many slightly different shapes. The degree of elongation (the ratio of the long axis to the short axis) is usually between 2.5 : 1 and 4 : 1, although a ratio of 60 : 1 has been recorded (**3.9**). The greater elongation of drumlins may well be associated with more powerful ice flow.

There is considerable discussion regarding the actual formation of drumlins. It is possible that they may be formed in a number of different ways:

■ By the lodgement of debris as it melts out of the basal ice layers.
■ By the reshaping of previously deposited ground moraine during a readvance phase.
■ By the accumulation of till around bedrock obstacles.
■ By a thinning of ice (as for example where a glacier spews out onto a lowland), which reduces the ability of the ice to carry all its load. Some is dumped, but continued forward movement of the ice streamlines and moulds the till that has already been deposited.
■ By friction between an ice sheet's ground deposits and the underlying bedrock, and where this friction is greater than the adhesion between those deposits and the ice. This is likely to encourage the ice to ruckle its ground deposits.
■ By catastrophic floods beneath ice sheets, which are capable of rippling ground moraine into mounds and hollows.

It is possible of course that each of the above explanations is valid, but only applies in particular areas. In short, it may be that there is no one universal mechanism for drumlin formation.

Drumlins are fairly rare over glaciated Europe, but here and there they are to be found in quite large numbers. In the British Isles, large concentrations of drumlins (often referred to as **swarms**) occur in north-west England and southern Scotland (**3.6**). But even more impressive is the great belt of drumlins that extends across nearly all of the northern half of Ireland. The world's largest drumlin field is to be found in New York State, where there are over 10 000 drumlins between Lake Ontario and the Finger Lakes.

Case study: A mix of drumlins in north-west England

In any one drumlin field, there are some interesting variations in drumlin elongation. In the drumlin belt of the Eden Valley and the Solway lowlands, the elongation of 100 drumlins varies between 1.1 : 1 and 9.7 : 1, with a mean elongation of 3.0 : 1 (**3.9**). The elongation of the drumlins is found to be greatest where the ice was moving fastest and the ice was thickest. This occurred in the area to the north of the Lake District around Wigton and Aspartia. The elongation also increases in the Tyne gap, where the ice was being squeezed through the gap and was flowing fast. Larger drumlins reach 100 m in height and up to 20 km in length, while the smallest are 2 m high and 10 m long. Drumlins also vary in composition. Most are formed of till, with the long axis of the rocks lying parallel to glacier flow. A few have a rock core, while others are composed largely of fluvioglacial deposits.

Figure 3.10 The distribution and elongation of drumlins in the Eden Valley and Solway lowlands

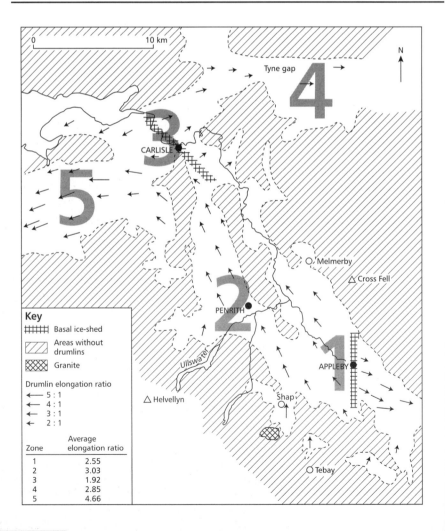

Key

▦	Basal ice-shed
▨	Areas without drumlins
▨	Granite

Drumlin elongation ratio
← 5 : 1
← 4 : 1
← 3 : 1
← 2 : 1

Zone	Average elongation ratio
1	2.55
2	3.03
3	1.92
4	2.85
5	4.66

Review

15 Which of the explanations of drumlin formation do you find most persuasive? Give your reasons.

16 Explain how the study of drumlins can throw important light on an area's history of glaciation.

This chapter needs to conclude with a strong word of warning. In it, we have examined the work of ice as a mover of load and depositor of load. What needs to be understood is that ice is rarely a sole operator. In many instances, it is working in conjunction with water, particularly meltwater. When this is the case, it becomes extremely difficult to isolate the work of one from the other. This point is well demonstrated by recessional moraines and drumlins. It is a vital point to bear in mind when reading the next chapter.

Enquiry

1   A photograph of Pjetursson's moraine can be found at

    http://www.geogr.ku.dk/as/Asuk-pjet.htm

    Identify the features that you can see in this picture and explain how they might have been formed.

2   Visit the home page of Copenhagen University's Geography Department, at

    http://www.geogr.ku.dk/

    Click on the icon for 'Snowmelt'. Run the animation and print off the accompanying notes. Write a short report on the processes and landscape changes in this area.

4

Proglacial environments

So far, we have considered only the direct work of ice. With advancing ice sheets and glaciers, that work largely involves picking up load, carrying it and remoulding it. That work continues even when ice sheets and glaciers are in retreat. This is because a forward motion is sustained even within retreating ice. But in retreat a new task is added, namely the deposition of load, and as a consequence the creation of wholly new landforms. Another significant change associated with retreat is the release of great quantities of meltwater. Actually, meltwater exists even within advancing warm-based glaciers, but the erosive and transportational power of that water increases tremendously when the ice front moves into reverse. Retreat involves unlocking some of the huge global reservoir of freshwater that is locked up in ice sheets and glaciers.

This chapter puts the spotlight on this meltwater. The term **fluvioglacial** (sometimes expressed the other way round, as **glaciofluvial**) is used to describe its processes and effects. Such activity occurs within and beneath the ice, and becomes increasingly important downstream from the **equilibrium line** (the boundary between the accumulation and ablation zones). But it is most active and its impacts are greatest immediately beyond the ice margin or glacier snout, in the area known as the **proglacial zone (4.1)**.

Figure 4.1 The snout of the Myrdalsjökull glacier, southern Iceland. Braided streams can be seen cutting across the sandur

Glacier hydrology

Meltwater is most abundant in warm-based glaciers, particularly where such glaciers are in retreat. In these glaciers, water may flow as a thick film between the solid rock and the base of the ice, thus enabling the glacier to move forward. Meltwater is derived in a number of ways:

- By **surface melting** – this is the most important source, but supply will vary both spatially and over time. Normally, melting will increase downstream as the glacier descends into areas of less severe climate. Aspect and orientation are influential, with south- and south-west-facing slopes receiving higher amounts of insolation. Clearly, melting will also vary between winter and summer, day and night.
- By **precipitation** – in some glacial basins, precipitation in the form of rain and snowmelt may enter the meltwater system as run-off down valley sides.
- By **geothermal heating** – small amounts of heat may be transferred from the bedrock to the base of the ice. In the Alps, bedrock temperatures of 1.5°C have been recorded underneath some glaciers. This is sufficient to cause melting at the base, particularly if the ice is at or close to the **pressure melting point**.
- By **mechanical heating** – heat is produced by the ice as it passes over and around obstacles, and also by internal friction or basal sliding. The amount of melting produced in these ways can be quite significant where there is rapidly moving ice at the pressure point.

There is a tendency to think of ice as a wholly solid mass, but in effect it behaves rather like limestone. It has both **primary** and **secondary permeability**. The former relates to the porosity of the upper layers of both snow and firn, which makes throughflow possible. As depth increases, the firn layer becomes impermeable as pores and fissures are sealed by frozen water or squeezed shut. Thus a sort of 'water table' is reached, below which throughflow is impossible. Secondary permeability refers to the network of tunnels, cavities and conduits that exist within most ice masses. Water is able to descend rapidly to the glacier base by means of these routeways (**4.2**). But even these can become choked by either winter ice or ice deformation.

Thus most glaciers and ice sheets are host to two largely independent 'drainage' systems. One involves surface water and the englacial water of layers near the surface.

Figure 4.2 The meltwater routes of a warm-based glacier

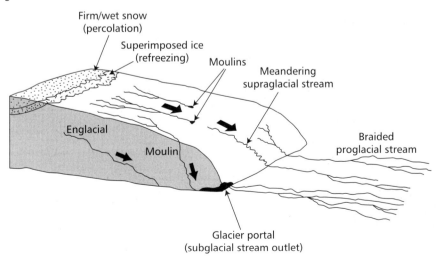

Firm/wet snow (percolation)

Superimposed ice (refreezing)

Moulins

Meandering supraglacial stream

Englacial

Moulin

Braided proglacial stream

Glacier portal (subglacial stream outlet)

The other involves subglacial water moving at the base of the ice. Initially, much of the water produced by surface melting moves supraglacially (**4.2**). On the glacier surface, it flows in a network of small rills and channels, often interrupted by pools. These channels are quite distinctive in that they meander freely and are typically 2 m wide. The surface is also pockmarked by sinks, known as **moulins**, and it is into these that many of the supraglacial streams tip their meltwater. By so doing, the meltwater enters the secondary permeability network of tunnels and cavities. The englacial flow of water is most active during summer months when these passageways become enlarged by melting and the greatly increased volume of meltwater.

Once it reaches the base of the ice, the meltwater that started at the surface meets up with the meltwater that has been produced by geothermal and mechanical heating, or that has entered the glacier as run-off running down the valley sides above the glacier. This basal water may flow as a thin film between the ice and the rock floor. In doing so, it acts as a lubricant, encouraging the glacier to move forward. Basal meltwater may also flow through tunnels, of which there are two types:

- **R-** (or **Rothlisberger**) **channels** – these are formed in basal ice where the bedrock provides a flat floor. They are believed to exist because the release of heat (presumably of geothermal origin) causes localised melting of the basal ice. Furthermore, it is assumed that the amount of heat is sufficient to melt enough ice to prevent the channel closing during the long winter months. Because the positions of these channels are constantly changing, it is believed that the subglacial streams running through them are unable to erode the bedrock into distinct channels.
- **N-** (or **Nye**) **channels** – these are cut by subglacial meltwater under high pressure. They are usually less than 1 m wide, sinuous, short and fragmented. In other words, they are not linked together into any sort of comprehensive channel network. Because they are generally more stable than the R-channels, streams running through them are able to erode channels in the bedrock. Because of this, it is believed that the bulk of subglacial meltwater moves through these rather than the R-tunnels.

Since the general direction of meltwater flow is downslope and therefore down the glacier, there comes a point at which it eventually emerges from under the ice. These points of exit are known as **portals (4.2)**. Naturally, they occur most frequently at the glacier snout or ice front.

Meltwater flows within and out of ice are highly variable. Discharge from glaciers has a marked diurnal pattern, being high during the day (especially when it is sunny) and low at night. The hydrograph is a regularly fluctuating one (**4.3a**). Daytime flow is often more than twice that at night. Indeed, it can often take on the appearance of a small daily flood. This can be hazardous for Alpine walkers, since streams that were easily

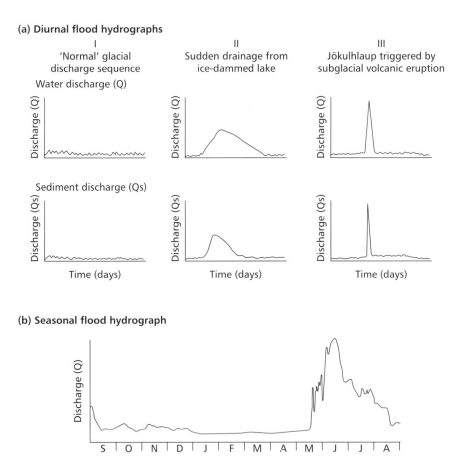

(a) Diurnal flood hydrographs

I
'Normal' glacial discharge sequence
Water discharge (Q)

II
Sudden drainage from ice-dammed lake

III
Jökulhlaup triggered by subglacial volcanic eruption

Sediment discharge (Qs)

Time (days)

(b) Seasonal flood hydrograph

Discharge (Q)

S O N D J F M A M J J A

Figure 4.3 Diurnal and seasonal variations in meltwater discharges

passable during the morning may become dangerous torrents in the afternoon. Even more hazardous are the jökulhlaups and floods caused by the breaching of ice-dammed lakes.

Meltwater discharge also varies seasonally (**4.3b**). The Glacier d'Argentiere in France, for example, has a winter discharge of 0.1–1.5 cumecs and a summer discharge of 10–11 cumecs. Until early summer, many of the flow routes are blocked by winter ice and snow. By late summer, however, a well-connected internal drainage system supports the large surface flow. By autumn, flows begin to decline and temperatures lower. Thus the meltwater hydrograph is a complicated one, with daily peaks and troughs superimposed on the on the rise and fall of seasonal flow.

Case study: Glacial outbursts

A glacial outburst is a short-lived and sometimes catastrophic flood resulting from the sudden release of meltwater stored within or on the surface of a glacier or ice sheet, or from a lake dammed up against the ice margin. Particularly large outbursts (known as **jökulhlaups**) are frequent in Iceland, where large quantities of meltwater result from normal ablation and the escape of geothermal heat beneath the ice in this volcanically active region.

One famous example is provided by the periodic outburst (every 10 years or so) of the large meltwater lake adjacent to the Grimsvötn caldera (collapsed volcano) located beneath the Vatnajökull ice cap, Europe's largest. Water builds up until it reaches a point at which it is able to escape via a tunnel in the ice that is 40 km in length. This causes spectacular flooding on the outwash plain beyond the ice cap margin. The volume of water discharged during these events averages out at between 3 and 3.5 km³. The 1922 jökulhlaup, when there was a total discharge of 7.1 km³ of water, remains one of the largest on record.

Figure 4.4 The Vatnajökull glacial outburst (1996)

Plate tectonics
Iceland straddles the Eurasian and American tectonic plates, which are moving away from each other. This leads to constant volcanic and earthquake activity.

Loki volcano
The eruption breaks through ice 600 m thick: the ice is melted to a depth of 250 m. The volcano is not cone-shaped, but is a huge fissure in the Earth's surface. The previous major eruption, which caused extensive flood damage, was in 1938.

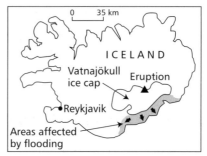

Vatnajökull ice cap
Vatnajökull is Europe's largest ice cap, covering an area 1900 km², and is up to 1.5 km deep in places. The name means 'water glacier'. There have been more than 50 eruptions since the Vikings settled Iceland in the 9th century.

Subglacial lake
The lake reaches its highest level in the 20th century, and covers an area of 7 km² to a depth of 100 m

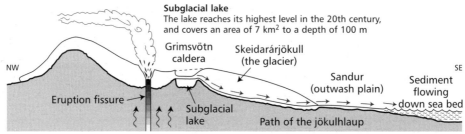

Heat from the volcano melts the glacier and puts pressure on the existing underground lake

The flood waters are carried towards the sea along channels and through a huge network of underground tunnels, causing widespread damage to roads, bridges and power lines, and threatening rich marine stocks by raising the temperature of coastal waters.

In September 1996, an earthquake measuring 5.0 on the Richter scale was recorded from within the Vatnajökull ice cap. This was followed by a swarm of smaller earthquakes. A volcanic fissure at Loki Ridge, just to the north-west of the Grimsvötn caldera, erupted on 2 October, and within a couple of days the ice cap had been pushed upwards by as much as 15 m by the melting of large volumes of ice. Up to 3 km3 of water was trapped beneath the ice cap. However, the expected jökulhlaup did not happen until early November. On the morning of the flood, the discharge of the Skeidarar River rose from 70 cumecs to 90 000 cumecs within a few hours. Luckily no lives were lost, but bridges and roads were destroyed. In addition to the flooding, the jökulhlaup also triggered further volcanic activity. As the trapped water escaped, so it released pressure on the Earth's surface, thus allowing the volcano to 'let off steam' in a flurry of minor eruptions.

Review

1 Explain the meaning of the term **fluvioglacial**.

2 Why is water important to a glacier?

3 Identify the main sources of glacial meltwater.

4 Describe and explain why meltwater flows vary from (a) place to place and (b) over time.

5 Outline the primary and secondary permeability characteristics of a glacier.

6 Distinguish between **R-** and **N-channels**.

7 Suggest reasons why the Vatnajökull jökulhlaup of 1996 did not cause any deaths.

SECTION B

Meltwater erosion and transportation

We have seen that glacial meltwater is distinguished by a number of characteristics. These include its varying levels of discharge, its turbulence and its ability to reach hazardously large proportions. Another, not mentioned as yet, is the **viscosity** (resistance to flow) of meltwater. Glacial meltwater is typically more viscous than normal river water. This is due to the fact that viscosity increases as temperatures fall, and the temperature of meltwater is typically closer to freezing point than most river water. This can have a considerable impact on the processes of transport and deposition. For example, viscous water is able to carry more material in suspension and to dislodge and entrain greater amounts of bedload. The **fall velocity** (that is, the velocity at which material of a given size is deposited) will also be lower in meltwater, so that more material will remain in suspension at lower velocities than in normal rivers. Clearly, this may be expected to have an impact on the rate and location of sedimentation.

The water film that exists between the base of the ice and the bedrock plays an important part in overall erosion, as it flushes out the **rock flour** produced by glacial erosion. There is also considerable chemical activity within that water film. Evidence for this is provided by measurements of the solute load of meltwater streams and small-scale surface features such as pitting. Meltwater is capable of attacking limestone and dolomite. At low temperatures, CO_2 becomes more soluble. This has the knock-on effect of making the meltwater more acidic and more aggressive in its ability to dissolve calcium. The weakening of the bedrock by chemical action will inevitably help to raise the rate of glacial and fluvioglacial erosion.

Most of the transportation undertaken by meltwater takes place during a relatively few weeks each year; that is, during the summer flood (**4.3b**). The relative proportions of bedload to suspended load vary with valley gradient and stream velocity. On steep slopes, bedload will be dominant. In all

Case study: The buried tunnel-valleys of East Anglia

Research by geomorphologists in East Anglia has revealed the existence of a network of channels, some of which are occupied by rivers today (**4.5**). They are typically quite deeply incised into the solid geology, but subsequently infilled with sand and gravel. Controversy surrounds their possible origins. To some, these **tunnel-valleys** (as they are called) were cut by the large amounts of meltwater flowing beneath the East Anglian ice sheets. Others are of the view that they are overdeepened glacial valleys, subsequently obliterated by drift. Still others argue that they are neither of these things but, rather, that they are ancient valleys of pre-glacial origin that were graded to a low sea level. Furthermore, they hold that these valleys have only been modified by localised glacial and subglacial activity.

Figure 4.5 The buried tunnel-valleys of East Anglia

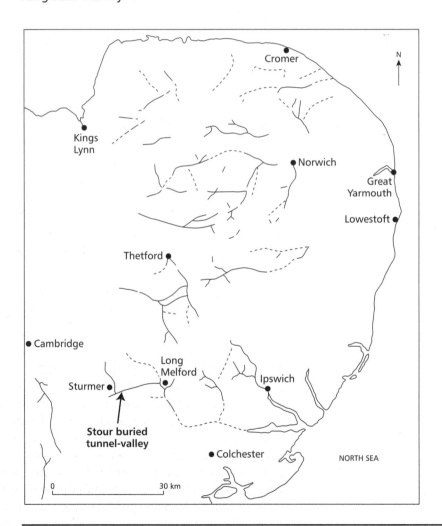

circumstances, the amount of load in suspension can be considerable, and the presence of dissolved load must not be overlooked.

The relatively large amount of load carried by meltwater increases the amount of mechanical erosion, especially of abrasion. For this reason alone, landforms associated with mechanical erosion are quite common in fluvioglacial environments. Pitting and etching of the water-worn surfaces are evidence of hydraulic action, while **sichelwannen** (crescent-shaped scour marks) and potholes up to 20 m deep are the outcomes of abrasion. Meltwater channels are another feature of erosion (see **Section D**). Newtondale in North Yorkshire is an excellent example of a huge overflow channel. It is perhaps difficult for us to realise that the slopes seen today simply show us the size of just the channel rather than its even larger encompassing valley. The power of meltwater erosion is also reflected in the deep, narrow channels cut into solid bedrock (**subglacial gorges**) beneath the ice. In post-glacial times, some of these have remained water-filled to give a type of ribbon lake, as at Loch Broom in Scotland and in the Glencoe area.

It is important for us to bear in mind all these characteristics in the discussion that follows, about the formation of fluvioglacial landforms.

Review

8 Summarise the main characteristics of meltwater.

9 Give reasons for the high rates of erosion achieved by meltwater.

10 Why does the composition of meltwater load depend on gradient?

SECTION C

Meltwater deposition

As with rivers, so with ice and meltwater: deposition will occur whenever the flow velocity diminishes. Material may be deposited as thin layers of silt, sand or gravel, as a channel-fill marking the site of a former stream, or as thick layers accumulated over many years. Fluvioglacial deposits can be differentiated from those laid down directly by the ice by their stratified nature (see **3.2b** on page 37). The sediments forming outwash plains, eskers, kames and other fluvioglacial features were laid down in environments dominated by:

- variable but often powerful meltwater flows
- the progressive collapse of ice through melting during retreat phases (**4.6**).

Outwash plains and valley trains

There are two major types of landform produced by meltwater deposition, depending on whether or not a glacier or ice sheet is involved and on local relief conditions. With a glacier hemmed in by steep valley walls, any outwash will be similarly confined. The resulting deposit is generally known as a **valley train**. But where there is a wide ice margin pushing out on to a broad lowland area, meltwater streams can spread widely, and likewise their load. It is in this way that extensive **outwash plains** (also known as **sandurs**) are formed. The coarsest materials (gravels) are dropped first near the ice margin, while the finer materials are carried further downslope, with clay and silt deposited last of all. Because of the strong seasonal variations in discharge, meltwater channels can easily become choked. In winter, the streams are unable to transport the same amount of load as in the summer months. As a consequence, their courses become braided.

Kettles or **kettle holes** are circular depressions in outwash plains and valley trains. They result from the gradual decay of detached blocks of ice left behind, as it were, by retreating glacier snouts and ice margins. Initially occupied by meltwater, they subsequently often become infilled with sands and gravels. Indeed, they are frequently buried by later sediments. Sometimes individual kettles coalesce to form quite large lakes.

Excellent examples of valley trains are to be found in southern Alaska and in the Southern Alps of New Zealand. Most valleys that have been glaciated show some evidence of having subsequently been modified by valley train development. An example of a vast outwash plain is provided by Luneberg Heath, on the German section of the North European Plain. Good examples are also to be found in the country that has provided the term **sandur** – Iceland.

Eskers

Eskers are elongated and winding ridges made up mainly of silts, sands and gravels (**4.6**). Coarser material is sorted and well rounded, the latter produced by vigorous attrition, particularly when meltwater is in full spate. Esker slopes are variable. At times they are steep, lying at the angle of rest of their component material, but in most cases they have subsequently been modified into gentler slopes of 5–10°. Even though they may be tens of kilometres long, large eskers are rarely wider than 800 m or higher than 50 m. The typical dimensions of an esker are 200–300 m long, 40–50 m wide and 10–20 m high.

How eskers are formed is not entirely clear. Two explanations are offered. One view is that they are made up of sediments that have built up within subglacial channels or tunnels. Deposition within ice tunnels would have occurred particularly where flow was impeded, perhaps due to the presence of a large lake at the ice margin whose surface level was higher than the tunnel exit. Equally, the build-up of sediment may reflect the choking of ice tunnels as meltwater stream discharges declined during the final stages of deglaciation.

Set against this is the view that any meltwater streams in those tunnels would have operated under very high-pressure conditions, and that such conditions would not have encouraged deposition. Rather, deposition would have occurred where such streams eventually emerged from beneath the ice and where they were no longer constrained. So, given a continuously retreating ice front and with the point of deposition therefore constantly moving backwards, the deposited load would gradually emerge as a linear ridge. Certainly, such a view of their formation would help to

Figure 4.6 The formation of eskers, kames and kame terraces

(a) Cross-section

1 During glaciation

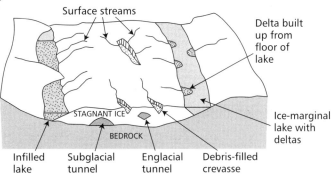

2 After glaciation

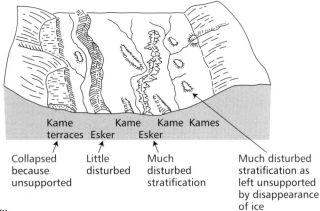

(b) Long profile

1 During glaciation

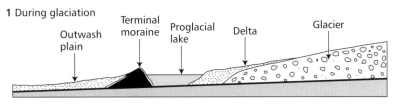

2 After glaciation

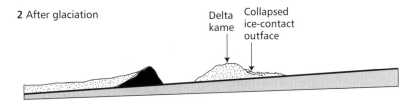

explain the occurrence of so-called **beaded eskers,** namely ridges showing frequent variations in width and height. The 'beads' of greater width and height might be seen as representing periods during which the rate of ice retreat either temporarily slowed or halted. Equally, the beads may be seen as the product of greatly increased deposition during the summer months.

Whatever the explanation of eskers may be in general, we are certainly justified in seeing them as the 'fossilised' casts of former subglacial meltwater streams. Some of the best eskers in the British Isles are to be found in the Trim area near Dublin. In all, there are 12 of them, but the most famous is the Trim esker itself. It is 14.5 km in length and increases in height southeastwards from 4 to 15 m, a height sustained for the last 8 km of its length. The formation of all the eskers in the area is related to the southeastward retreat of the central Irish ice cap some 10 000 years ago.

Kames and kame terraces

Kames are mounds of sand and gravel that have been deposited in a number of different ways (**4.6**):

- as deltas laid down by meltwater streams flowing into lakes that were held up at the ice margins
- as accumulations in shallow depressions, worn in thin ice by supraglacial meltwater, that have subsequently melted out
- as deposit-filled ice crevasses that simply collapsed as mounds when the ice finally disappeared.

Because of these diverse origins, kames can assume many different forms, from chaotic assemblages of knolls and depressions to groups of flat-topped, roughly parallel mounds.

Kame terraces are more continuous fluvioglacial features created along the lateral margins of ice (**4.6**). In the field, they are recognised as ridges of sand and gravel running along the sides of valleys. They are deposited by meltwater streams flowing along the junction between the glacier and the exposed valley side. Small troughs are formed at this junction because the exposed valley side heats up faster, and more than the glacier ice. The result is a melting of the ice in immediate contact with the warmer hillside. In some cases, the trough can become a linear lake. In general appearance, kame terraces differ little from lateral moraines, but the all important difference lies in the component material – sorted in the former, unsorted in the latter.

East Lothian in Scotland is an area rich in kames and kame terraces. The terraces here reach up to 1.5 km in length and 200 m in width, but most kames are only a few hundred metres long and tens of metres wide. The kame terraces can be traced as occurring at four distinct levels between 245 and 320 m O.D. The kame surfaces are mostly flat. They are mainly formed of sand and gravel but, in some, clay and silt also occur.

Varves

The floors of many lakes close to ice margins are covered by distinctive deposits known as **varves**. These typically comprise an alternating sequence of coarser (sand and gravel) and finer (clay and silt) bands. The coarser sediment is that which has been deposited in summer when

Review

11 Explain the link between seasonal meltwater flows and the braiding of stream channels.

12 Summarise the different views of esker formation. Which do you prefer, and why?

13 Distinguish between a **kame** and a **kame terrace**.

14 Draw simple annotated diagrams to show the different origins of kames.

15 Check that you understand the link between varve thickness and climate.

meltwater discharges are high; the finer sediment is that which slowly settles out during the winter, when little or no coarse sediment is being washed into the lake. Thus each pair of varves represents a year's accumulation. The age (or duration of existence) of the lake can therefore be discovered by counting the varves on the lake floor.

The varve deposits for individual years tend to vary somewhat in thickness, according to the year's weather and its effects on the rates of transport and deposition. Thus fluctuations in the relative thickness of varves can provide information about climate change by indicating periods of warming (thickening) and cooling (thinning).

The modification of drainage

Pre-existing drainage systems are rarely completely obliterated, or even radically changed, by the actions of glacial and fluvioglacial processes. Indeed, in glaciated uplands, glacier movement may be largely guided by pre-existing valleys, and it is only when these prove inadequate to deal with the mass of ice that new courses might be cut, perhaps even across watersheds and interfluves. In contrast, the massive ice sheets of lowland areas may be much less influenced by the pre-existing patterns of relief and drainage. For example, the main direction of ice advance in many parts of the British Isles was transverse to river valleys and their divides. But rather than being obliterated, such features have remained largely 'ignored' and therefore intact beneath the ice. Equally, it has to be admitted that the vast amounts of meltwater present in the proglacial zone during the retreat stages must have, to varying degrees, modified the drainage features of the pre-glacial landscape.

Proglacial lakes are recognised as being a regular occurrence at the margins of retreating glaciers and ice sheets (**4.7**). They are seen as being formed by meltwater trapped between that margin and higher ground created by recessional or terminal moraines. Although many of those lakes left towards the end of the last ice age have since lost their waters and disappeared, it may be possible to reconstruct them using three pieces of field evidence:

- the former strand or shorelines of these lakes
- the deltaic deposits that were laid down in them by the meltwater streams of the time
- the steep-sided and often deeply entrenched channels (referred to as **meltwater channels** or **spillways**) cut by the meltwater as it escaped from lake to lake or away from the proglacial zone altogether.

It has to be said that some doubt has been cast on the origins of these channels. The problem is that many of these channels in upland Britain have 'humped' (up-and-down) long profiles. In other words, the channel floor slopes away in opposite directions from a high point. The same

Figure 4.7 The formation of proglacial lakes and meltwater channels

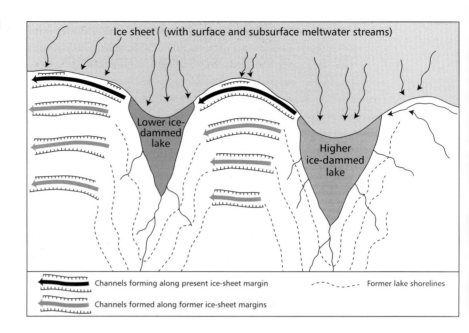

Ice sheet ((with surface and subsurface meltwater streams)

Lower ice-dammed lake

Higher ice-dammed lake

Channels forming along present ice-sheet margin

Channels formed along former ice-sheet margins

Former lake shorelines

characteristic is found in some eskers, which appear to climb up one side of a ridge and descend the other. As a result, there is a growing belief that these channels are the result of subglacial erosion, by water flowing in tunnels at the base of the ice. It is argued that the meltwater was under such great hydrostatic pressure that it could be forced to run uphill and erode at the same time. If this is true, then these channels are the erosional counterparts of eskers.

In conclusion, it should now be clear that the proglacial zone is an important cold environment. Part of that importance is due to the simple fact that, as ice sheets and glaciers retreat, so the proglacial zone widens. In doing so, the glaciated landscape is progressively encroached upon by fluvioglacial processes. Gradually, it can become considerably modified by the vast amounts of meltwater that are available on a fluctuating daily and seasonal basis. But the outcomes of that meltwater modification are predominantly depositional rather than erosional. Looking in the other direction, we should remember that this same depositional work has been responsible for masking large areas never touched by glaciation.

Review

16 Summarise the arguments about overflow channels.

Study **4.8**, which shows a retreating glacier in Iceland.

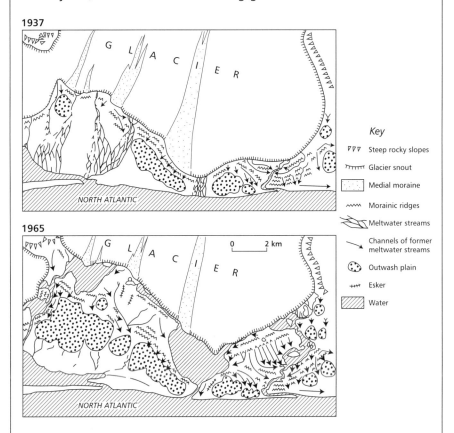

Figure 4.8 A retreating glacier in Iceland

1 Describe the changes that have taken place on the outwash plain.

2 Describe and explain the changing pattern of morainic ridges.

3 Comment on the location of eskers. Suggest how they may have been formed.

Periglacial environments

Today, nearly a quarter of the world's land area is estimated as having a climate that cannot be described as 'glacial', in that it does not sustain ice sheets and glaciers, and yet is characterised by long periods of extreme cold and winter snowfall. Such 'arctic' conditions are widespread in the Northern Hemisphere, where they are associated with the tundra regions of Alaska and northern Canada, coastal Greenland, extreme northern Europe and a great swathe of Siberia. As will be explained shortly, the map of permafrost distribution (**5.1**) gives a general indication of the main periglacial regions. However, it is necessary to point out that the conditions are also experienced at lower latitudes, but of course only at high altitudes, as in the Alps, the Tibetan Plateau and sections of the high Andes.

It was the Polish geologist Walery von Lozinski who, in 1909, first introduced the term 'periglacial' to describe frost weathering conditions that had led to the creation of the great rock screes found in the Carpathian Mountains. He later broadened the term to include the climate and geomorphology of areas adjacent to ice sheets and glaciers. However, geographers today see the periglacial 'package' as being even larger, embracing not just distinctive climatic features, processes and landforms, but also ecosystems that have cleverly adjusted to those physical conditions. The conditions allow a more diverse flora and fauna than is found in the glacial and proglacial environments considered in earlier chapters. There is also another aspect that sets the periglacial environment apart from the two previous. It has a human geography that is much more than the tourism and scientific research that marks the polar areas of ice sheets and glaciers. This point is taken further in **Chapter 6**.

SECTION A

Climatic characteristics

In Köppen's global classification of climates, periglacial areas fall mainly in the ET (tundra) category, but they also occur in parts designated as Df (cold temperate, no dry season). The climatic regime of these areas shows the following characteristics:

- A large annual range of temperature, with mean monthly temperatures ranging from –15°C to 10°C. However, during clear, calm weather, winter temperatures may fall to below –50°C, and in summer rise to over 20°C.

1 a Collect climatic
  data (mean
  monthly
  temperature,
  precipitation and
  wind speed) for
  one
  meteorological
  station in each of
  the following
  locations: north
  Alaska, Greenland
  and the Arctic
  coast of Russia.

 b Represent the
  data in graph
  form.

 c To what extent are
  the four
  generalisations in
  Section A
  confirmed by your
  chosen stations?

■ Temperature patterns are related to the distribution of land and sea. In summer, Arctic land masses are warmer than the surrounding oceans and maritime regions. Melting pack ice helps to keep temperatures in check around 0°C, whereas continental areas are less affected and therefore become warmer. The situation is reversed in winter.

■ Precipitation is rarely more than 250 mm a year, and a significant amount of this falls as sleet or snow. This relative aridity is largely due to persistently low air temperatures. Cold air is only able to hold small amounts of moisture. Persistent high-pressure conditions also help to reduce the amount of rainfall. In the summer months, however, depressions associated with the polar front move polewards and these can bring considerable amounts of rain and sleet. Rainfall, and for that matter precipitation as a whole, decline away from oceans, as the westerly depressions progressively lose moisture as they travel inland.

■ Winds are significant in that they are typically strong. There are a number of obvious consequences. Wind has to be reckoned with as an agent of denudation (eroding, transporting and depositing). It is also effective in redistributing snow and, in particular, in creating sizeable drift accumulations. The wind chill factor here is capable of lowering sensible temperatures to hazardous levels.

It is the combination of persistent sub-freezing temperatures and low precipitation (in other words, reasonably clear skies) that makes severe frost such a distinguishing feature of the periglacial climatic regime. A second characteristic – the prevalence of ground that is frozen for all or much of the year – is the outcome of the long and bitterly cold winters. While winters may be long, summers short and the intermediate seasons even shorter, the spring and autumn are particularly important in terms of landform development. We will pick up this last point in **Section C**.

SECTION B

Permafrost

Without question, the most important single feature of the periglacial environment is the deep permanent freezing of the subsoil and underlying rock. Such frozen ground is known as **permafrost**. It is calculated that in order for permafrost to develop, the mean annual temperature must be as low as –4°C. Where temperatures are below this threshold, the frozen ground may reach to great depths. Today, the permafrost of Alaska and Siberia reaches to depths of over 300 m. A depth of over 1500 m has been claimed at one location in Siberia.

At this point, it is necessary to draw attention to the fact that three different types of permafrost are recognised (**5.1**):

■ **Continuous permafrost** is where the upper limit of the permafrost effectively remains at the ground surface throughout the year. There is very little, if any, surface melting during the summer months. For this reason, there is little weathering or erosion. Such areas are found

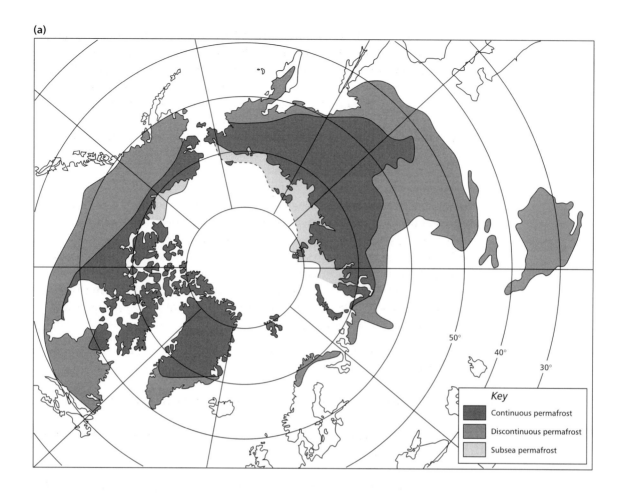

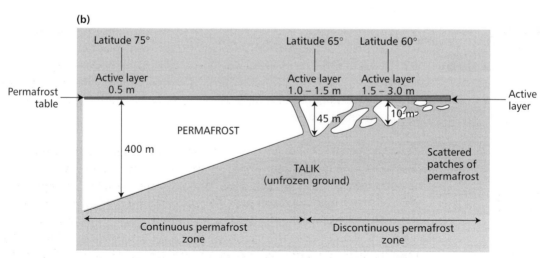

Figure 5.1 Permafrost in the Northern Hemisphere: (a) distribution; (b) cross-section

almost entirely within the Arctic Circle, except that in the continental interiors of North America and Eurasia the limit bulges southwards.

- **Discontinuous permafrost** is characterised by applying the adjective in two ways, namely to indicate that there is significant surface melting in the summer, and that the permafrost is fragmented by the existence of 'warmer' areas, such as those located close to rivers, lakes and coasts.
- **Subsea permafrost** reminds us that seabed deposits on bedrock beneath the shallower parts of the Arctic Ocean are also subject to permafrost conditions.

In terms of landform processes and development, the most significant aspect of the permafrost zone and profile is the surface layer that melts during the summer months. This is known as the **active layer** (5.1). Essentially, this layer increases in thickness with distance from the poles until the point is reached at which conditions are too warm for permafrost to exist at all. The active layer can vary in depth from a few centimetres to several metres. Latitude and altitude are not the only factors controlling the depth limit. Others include:

- **rock type** – coarse gravels thaw more quickly than clays
- **aspect** – the direction of slope has a considerable effect on insolation receipts
- **the presence or absence of an 'insulating' peaty soil** – this reduces thawing
- **the nature of the vegetation cover** – coniferous trees and shrubs shade the soil from sunlight.

Three aspects of the active layer are important in the context of landform development:

- the meltwater saturation of the ground above the permafrost table, which makes it highly mobile
- the opportunity for seasonal and diurnal cycles of alternating freeze–thaw to operate, thereby encouraging a major landform process
- the formation of ground ice when winter comes and the saturated ground freezes.

The direct effects of permafrost on landform development are negligible, for frozen ground is essentially inert ground. Indirectly, however, permafrost is a major influence on landform processes. For example, the freezing of ground makes it impermeable. Underground circulation of water is impossible. During the summer, when the winter snows and the upper ground thaw, there is an abundance of meltwater. On flat or gently undulating ground, the topmost layers become waterlogged and lead to the formation of marshes, pools and thaw lakes. On slopes, the permafrost table provides a 'slide' down which mass movements are encouraged.

If one drills deep enough into permafrost, eventually there comes a point at which the ground is no longer permanently frozen (5.1). This unfrozen ground is known as **talik**.

Review

2 Can you think of any other factors (apart from the six mentioned) that might affect the depth of the active layer?

3 Explain why frozen ground is described as 'inert'.

4 How might you explain the existence of talik under the permafrost?

Permafrost throughout Europe is melting, even to the point of threatening alpine villages and ski resorts with rockfalls and landslides. In parts of Switzerland, ground temperatures have risen by between 0.5 and 1°C over the past 15 years. During the same period, the number of reported landslides and avalanches has risen considerably.

Figure 5.2 A flow diagram of the periglacial system

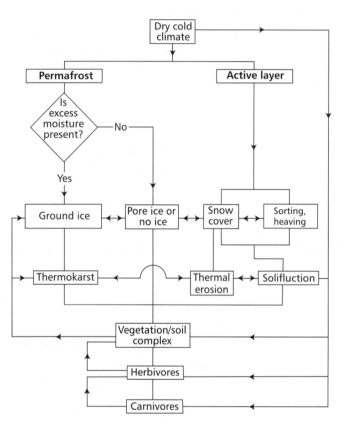

The PACE (Permafrost and Climate in Europe) organisation was set up in 1997 to monitor the creeping impact of climate change on the stability of mountain slopes. The combination of ground temperatures only slightly below freezing, high ice contents and steep slopes makes the mountain permafrost in Europe particularly vulnerable to even the smallest amount of climate change. Permafrost exists as far south as the summit areas of the Sierra Nevada in southern Spain. In the Alps, it is found above 2500 m; in the Scandinavian highlands the threshold is around 1500 m, whilst in Svalbard it starts at sea level.

Any further thawing of the permafrost will pose a threat not just to settlements, but to the whole infrastructure of tourism, particularly that related to winter sports. The twin fears are reduced slope stability and the 'settling' of buildings, roads, bridges and ski lifts, as load-bearing capacities are reduced by the deepening of the active layer (see **Chapter 6, Section C**).

SECTION C

Ground ice

A diagram of the periglacial system gives due prominence to the permafrost and the active layer (**5.2**). At the next level of significance comes the formation of ground ice within the active layer, particularly during the long winter freeze. It is the fact that water expands as it freezes that makes the formation of ground ice such a powerful force in landform development.

Pingos

Ground ice can take a number of different forms across a range of scales, from small ice needles (**pipkraker**) to large lenses of almost pure ice (**pingos**). The latter are perhaps the best known of the periglacial landforms. They are rounded ice-cored hills that can reach up to over 50 m in height and over 500 m in diameter. They come in two types (**5.3**). **Open system pingos** form in valley bottoms where water collects, freezes and forms large ice masses that heave up overlying sediments into domes. **Closed system pingos** develop beneath small lakes and lake beds. As permafrost grows, groundwater beneath the lake is trapped by freezing from above and from freezing inwards from the edge of the lake basin. The trapped groundwater thus forms a talik, which is increasingly compressed by the expanding ice surrounding it. As a result, the overlying sediments are gradually forced upwards. The end result is that the talik itself freezes to give an ice-cored dome.

Figure 5.3 The formation of pingos

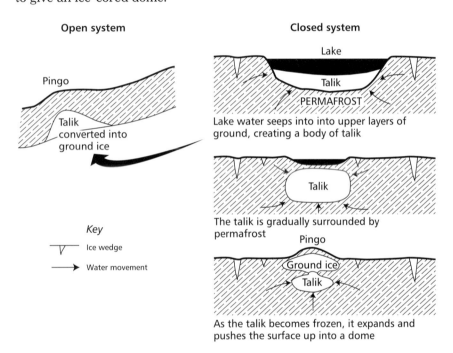

Probably one of the best assemblages of pingos is found in the Mackenzie delta in Canada, where some 1400 have been identified. Relict pingos can be found in parts of the British Isles, as for example in the Vale of Llanberis (Wales). However, they do not appear today as rounded hillocks. Because the ice core has long since thawed out, the domes have collapsed to leave a pond or depression surrounded by ramparts.

Ice wedges and patterned ground

An ice wedge is mass of ground ice that tapers downwards from the surface. They develop at points at which summer meltwater penetrates the ground via open fissures and then, with the onset of winter, subsequently freezes and expands. Over years, with the regular alternation of thawing and freezing, so the penetrating ice assumes a wedge shape, becoming wider and deeper. Annual growth rates downward vary between 1 and 20 mm. Over a long period of time, wedges may reach a depth of 10 m. At the top, they are rarely more than 1.5 m in width. Fossil ice wedges are found in areas now enjoying a warmer climate. The ice has melted and the space infilled with sands and gravels. A good example is the Long Hanborough Carrot near Oxford.

Where the active layer undergoes severe winter freezing (with clear winter skies allowing temperatures to drop to –20°C), the ground contracts and cracks (referred to as **thermal contraction**). Not only do the cracks develop into ice wedges, but at the surface they are arranged in rectangular patterns known as **ice-wedge polygons**. The raised ice at the surface of each wedge means that the centres of the polygons are lower and often occupied by surface water.

What is known as **patterned ground** is formed in a similar way, but in areas where precipitation is low and there is not enough water to form significant masses of ice. Thermal contraction, along with desiccation cracking, produce the same polygonal network of fissures and cracks, but instead of ice they are infilled with sand and gravel. There is both a vertical and a lateral sorting of the material, and this results in larger stones moving upwards and outwards to the margins of the polygon, while fine-grained material gathers at the centre. The term **stone circle** is an apt description of this type of patterned ground. In the general terms, polygons and circles develop best on level ground. On slopes, the same processes are at work, but the resulting shapes are distorted by process of mass movement (see **solifluction** below; see also **5.4**). On particularly steep or mobile slopes, the stone margins may become so distorted as to appear as **stone stripes**.

Thermokarst

Where there is extensive thawing of ground ice, as for example by fire or during a period of climatic warming, a highly irregular surface of hummocks, shallow depressions, pits and troughs may be formed. Because its appearance is reminiscent of some forms of limestone terrain, such ground is referred to as **thermokarst**. The processes involved in creating this thermokarst include:

- the thawing of ice wedges to leave elongated depressions
- the thawing of pingo ice cores to produce circular depressions with raised rims
- the lateral movement of streams, leading to the exposure and melting of ground ice.

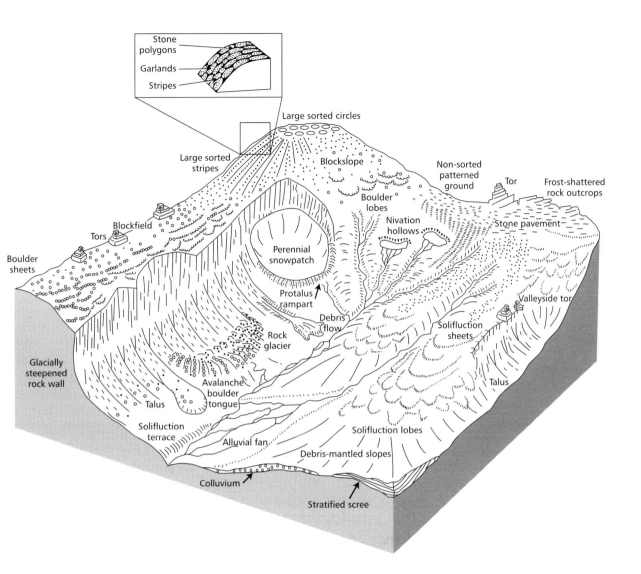

Figure 5.4 A periglacial landscape

The labels in the figure:

Stone polygons
Garlands
Stripes

Large sorted circles

Large sorted stripes

Blockslope

Non-sorted patterned ground

Tor

Frost-shattered rock outcrops

Boulder lobes

Nivation hollows

Stone pavement

Tors

Blockfield

Boulder sheets

Perennial snowpatch

Protalus rampart

Debris flow

Valleyside tor

Solifluction sheets

Glacially steepened rock wall

Rock glacier

Talus

Talus

Avalanche boulder tongue

Solifluction terrace

Alluvial fan

Solifluction lobes

Debris-mantled slopes

Colluvium

Stratified scree

Review

5 Check that you fully understand how the freeze–thaw process works.

6 In what ways do ice-wedge polygons differ from stone circles?

7 Can you think of any other circumstances that would result in the extensive thawing needed for the formation of thermokarst?

Other processes

It is the combination and intensity of processes that set the periglacial landscape apart from others. The presence of permafrost is of vital importance here. It provides an impermeable layer that prevents the downward percolation of water, keeping it at the surface or in the active layer. We have also seen that the regular alternation of freezing and thawing, particularly of ground ice, is no less critical. Under the name of **frost action**, that same daily and seasonal cycle of heating and cooling causes the intense weathering of jointed and porous rocks. Solid rock is gradually broken down to create blockfields, screes and frost-shattered cliffs and tors (**5.4**). But there are other effective processes at work moulding the periglacial landscape. Let us look at these.

Solifluction

While frost action is the chief process in preparing bedrock for erosion, solifluction is the main means of transporting the weathered material. Solifluction literally means flowing soil. It usually involves the slow downslope movement of weathered debris saturated by meltwater. The only pull factor as such is gravity. Provided that there is a high degree of saturation in the surface layers, solifluction can take place on quite gentle slopes (2–3°). Clearly, the steeper the slope and the higher the saturation, the greater will be the speed and volume of movement. The competence of solifluction is also increased where the permafrost table provides a surface down which weathered material can easily slide.

In some instances, the downslope movement of material in periglacial areas is helped by **frost creep**, which involves the displacement of slope particles by freeze–thaw action. When sloping ground freezes, frost heave will raise surface materials at right angles to the slope, but having been raised they will subsequently settle down vertically. The net effect is to move material slowly downslope.

Solifluction, along with frost creep and rainwash, slowly transport debris to the valley bottom, where it may either accumulate or be removed by a stream. In the former case, extensive sheets of debris (**solifluction sheets**) will gradually build up on the lower sections of the slope (**5.4**). There may come a time when the accumulation is so thick that the sheet becomes unstable. At this point, the debris will slump forward either as lobes (**solifluction lobes**) or terracettes (**solifluction terraces**).

Running water

Running water, the chief source of erosional transport in mid-latitudes, is of considerably less importance in periglacial environments. The reasons are threefold:

- low precipitation
- streams remain frozen for much of the year

- the presence of permafrost hinders channel development.

Nonetheless, most periglacial areas have drainage networks. Whilst they are similar in form to those found in temperate environments, there are two significant differences:

- The streams flow for only a short time each year, and because of this the accumulation of debris on valley floors exceeds the ability of streams to remove it. The characteristic braiding of many periglacial streams is probably evidence of this.
- Given the rapid melting of winter snowfall, periglacial streams frequently flood, and in that condition they appear to be quite capable of impressive vertical downcutting.

Nivation

Nivation (or **snowpatch erosion**, as it is sometimes termed) is responsible for the formation of rounded hollows, most often at valley heads (**5.4**). Nivation is really a collection of interacting processes acting beneath and at the edges of a snowpatch that has accumulated in some sort of initial depression in a hillside (**5.5**). The processes include:

- freeze–thaw action
- solifluction
- transport by running water
- possibly chemical weathering.

Figure 5.5 The formation of (a) nivation hollows and (b) cirques

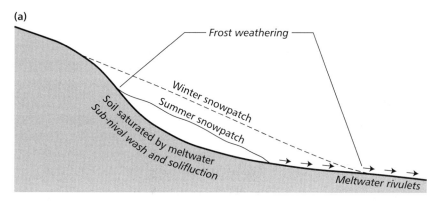

(a)

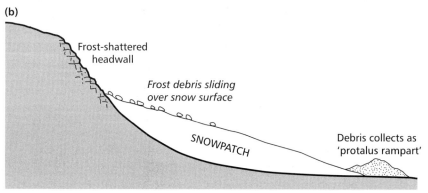

(b)

With seasonal enlargement and shrinkage of the snowpatch, surrounding areas will be subjected to frost action. The resulting debris will be removed, mainly in the summer, by solifluction and meltwater escaping from the foot of the ice. Over a long period, the snowpatch will slowly 'eat back' into the hillside, thus forming a rounded hollow with a comparatively steep headwall. In time, this nivation hollow may be so enlarged that it assumes the character of a cirque (**nivation cirque**).

Wind action

Strong winds are a feature of the periglacial climate, but their role is one of transport and deposition rather than erosion. Wind action is responsible for picking up large quantities of fine sediments produced by frost action and by glacial and fluvioglacial processes. This removal of sediments is most effective in areas of low relief and sparse vegetation cover, and particularly where conditions are very cold and dry. Towards the end of the last ice age, wind removed huge amounts of silt from the extensive outwash plains built in the proglacial zone. The silt was transported over long distances and eventually deposited as layers of **loess** (also known as **limon** in Western Europe).

Review

8   What is the difference between **freeze–thaw action** and **frost action?**

9   Think of some other factors that might affect the rate of solifluction.

10 In what ways might the evidence about river action in periglacial environments appear to be contradictory?

11 How does a **nivation cirque** differ from a **glacial cirque?**

12 Find out where the main deposits of **limon** occur in Western Europe. How do these areas lie in relation to the southward limit of glaciation?

Relict landscapes

Figure **5.1** gives a clear indication of the broad areas in the Northern Hemisphere that currently experience periglacial conditions. We also know that those same conditions were experienced much further south during the last ice age. Certainly, there is a considerable amount of evidence that periglacial environments were quite widespread in the British Isles. Nowhere is that evidence stronger than in the Chalk downlands of southern England. Here we may draw attention to a number of relict features:

■   **Coombe rock** is the name given to the deposits of frost-shattered and soliflucted chalk debris that are found in hollows cut into the scarp faces of the Chilterns and South Downs. The hollows are assumed to be nivation hollows excavated by snowpatch erosion.

■   **Dry valleys** are quite deeply cut valleys that are not occupied by rivers today. They are commonly found on chalk and limestone outcrops. An explanation of their formation assumes that they were cut, during periglacial times, by floods of spring meltwater that lowered valley floors rendered impermeable by permafrost. With the cessation of

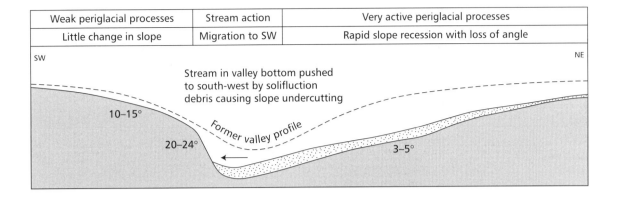

| Weak periglacial processes | Stream action | Very active periglacial processes |
| Little change in slope | Migration to SW | Rapid slope recession with loss of angle |

SW

Stream in valley bottom pushed to south-west by solifluction debris causing slope undercutting

10–15°

Former valley profile

20–24°

3–5°

NE

Figure 5.6 The formation of an asymmetrical valley

periglacial conditions, the permafrost melted, the streams disappeared underground and their valleys were left dry.

- **Misfit rivers** are relatively small streams and rivers that occupy large valleys. Rivers such as the Windrush and Evenlode in the Cotswolds are too small and too ineffective today to have created the deep valleys and wide flood plains that they presently occupy. However, during periglacial times, rapid run-off from snowmelt would have allowed them to carve such valleys.
- **Asymmetrical valleys** are common on Chalk dip slopes, particularly if their general trend is east–west. The south-facing slopes of such valleys received more insolation and were therefore subjected to more mass wasting than the north-facing slopes on the other side of the valley. Hence they were lowered and became more gently inclined (**5.6**). Accentuating the contrast between the two sides of the valley was the 'pushing' of the stream by solifluction deposits against the steeper north-facing side. The undercutting would also have helped to steepen the slope.
- **Solifluction terraces**, such as those at Maiden Castle in Dorset, are narrow step-like features known locally as 'sheep walks'. There is no disputing the periglacial origins of these widespread features.
- **Screes** and **blockfields** are well-developed features in many parts of upland Britain. All are agreed that, whilst they are the product of frost action, the level of such activity today would not be capable of producing features of such size. In short, they must have developed under periglacial conditions.

Review

13 Can you think of any reasons why the relict features of periglaciation in the British Isles should be most evident on chalk and limestone outcrops?

SECTION F

The tundra biome

Relative to other global biomes, the tundra is distinguished by low net plant productivity, low biodiversity and small populations of both plants and animals (**5.7**). The harsh climate hardly offers any alternative; nor do the poor soils. In many respects, the tundra is closely akin to the desert biome that prevails close to the Equator. The lower part of **5.2** (page 68) has already shown how the biome (its soils, vegetation and animals) is integrated in the periglacial system.

Soils

Soils in periglacial environments are strongly affected by permafrost. This, and the low temperatures, are the dominant factors in soil formation. Bacterial activity is low and waterlogging leads to the formation of an acid humus called **mor**. Just a few centimetres below the surface, a blue–grey blotchy mud is found, formed by the process of gleying. Ferric compounds are reduced into ferrous compounds as waterlogging causes the loss of oxygen. It is this that causes the blotchiness. Typically, soils contain angular fragments of rock resulting from freeze–thaw action and frost heave. On the better-drained land, podsols, with their distinct horizons, may develop.

Flora

Despite the low net plant productivity of the tundra biome (**5.7**), the plants found there do show a number of different and ingenious ways of coping with the harsh conditions (**5.8**). In this vein, another distinguishing feature of the flora is the existence within the biome of a number of different plant communities, each finely tuned to a different set of physical circumstances. These range from the moorland communities of the higher and better-drained land to the grass and sedge communities found in lower-lying and damper areas. In particularly favoured areas, dwarf shrubs such as willow and birch are to be found.

Towards the poles, the climate becomes drier and even colder, and summers are shorter. Plant cover and plant height decrease to the point at which it is appropriate to talk in terms of the **polar desert**. Here, less than 10 per cent of the surface area is vegetated, although locally – in favoured locations – moss and lichen may cover quite large areas. In Antarctica, there is a very limited cover of lichen, a few mosses survive in crevices and as a consequence soils lack organic material.

Figure 5.7 The net plant productivity of biomes

Biome	NPP $(g\ m^{-2}\ yr^{-1})$
Polar desert	0–1
Tropical desert	10–250
Arctic tundra	**100–400**
Temperate grassland	100–1500
Boreal forest	200–1500
Tropical savanna	400–2000
Deciduous forest	600–2500
Tropical rainforest	1000–3500

Fauna

Animal life in the tundra shows a number of distinguishing characteristics. These include the following:

- low biodiversity – there are nearly 9000 bird species in the world but only 70 breed in the Arctic, and of some 3200 mammals in the world only 23 occur in the Arctic
- large numbers of a single species, as for example of caribou, lemmings and certain seabirds
- population numbers are very cyclical, going through alternating phases of growth and decline – for example, lemming populations seem to oscillate over a cycle of 3–7 years.

The migrant birds, such as waders and buntings, that come to breed on the tundra during the short summer are particularly interesting. Why do they fly thousands of miles each year from their wintering grounds much nearer the Equator just to spend a month or two at these high latitudes? The

Figure 5.8 Plant adaptations to the tundra environment

Adaptation	Explanation
Prostrate shrubs	Insulation beneath snow, creating a warmer microclimate
Cushion plants	A warm microclimate created within the cushion up to 25°C warmer than the surrounding air
Herbaceous perennials	A large underground root structure stores food over winter
Rarity of annuals	The growing season is too short for the full cycle
Reproduction often by rhizomes, bulbs or layering	This avoids reliance on completing the flower–seed production cycle
Pre-formed flower buds	This maximises the time for seed production
Growth at low temperatures	This maximises the length of the growing season
Optimum photosynthesis	This maximises the rate of growth at low temperatures
Frost resistance	This applies to flowers, fruits and seeds
Longevity	Once established, the ability to prevail
Drought resistance	Suitable for growth on rock surfaces

Figure 5.9 Animal adaptations to the tundra environment

Environmental characteristic	Adaptation
Severe climate	A small number of species; low mean densities
Low temperatures	A high quality of insulation (e.g. fur, feathers); increased metabolic rates
Snow	Some small mammals are able to survive below snow; large herbivores are able to browse where the snow is thin and soft
Short summer, long winter	The breeding cycle is compressed
Low food supply	Birds and larger mammals migrate; litters and clutches are large

answer lies in food supply. Despite the short summer, there is an abundance of food in terms of insects, berries and seeds. Not only that, but this food is available 24 hours a day, thanks to the virtual absence of darkness.

In showing a typical food chain of the tundra, **5.10** shows something of the close and intricate interconnections that ensure the survival of life in this harsh, cold environment. Two rather more specific points are also brought into focus by the diagram. One concerns the importance of the sea to that wildlife survival. Plankton-rich seas support large populations of fish that, in turn, sustain huge seabird colonies along the coasts. The other point relates to the inclusion of people in the food chain. It reminds us that of all the cold environments, the periglacial is the one most colonised by people, albeit rather sparsely. It is not to overstate the situation to suggest that the future survival or destruction of this environment lies very much in human hands. As such, this provides a cue for the next and final chapter.

Figure 5.10 The tundra food chain

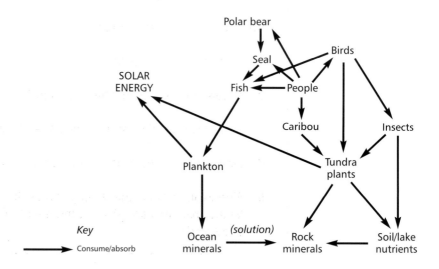

Review

14 Explain the possible relationship between soil, drainage and slope in the tundra.

15 Write a short account illustrating ways in which plants and animals have adapted to prevailing conditions in the tundra.

16 Study **5.10** and trace through the different ways in which people might upset the tundra food chain.

The highland interior of Greenland suffers a severe polar climate and the signs of wildlife are little more than lichens. However, the coastal regions, with their tundra climate, offer a slightly more encouraging environment.

Greenland's tundra vegetation is typically stunted. In sheltered areas around Qaqortoq and Narsarsuaq, for example, there are stands of dwarf birch, alder, juniper and willow. In late summer, the lowland areas of the south are covered with broad-leaf willow. Flowering plants include camomile, dandelion, harebell, buttercup, saxifrage and arctic cotton. Berried shrubs, such as huckleberry, crowberry and cranberry, are quite abundant. Mosses, sedges, grasses and lichens are widespread.

Due to the harsh conditions, Greenland's faunal life is sparse. Land mammals grade in size from polar bears through caribou, wolves, foxes, hares and so on down to lemmings.

Over 50 bird species breed on or near the shores. Among them are cormorants, puffins, guillemots, eider ducks, sea eagles, skuas, kittiwakes, divers and swans. Their main food supply lies in the rich North Atlantic waters rather than the periglacial tundra.

Nevertheless, the tundra does attract a limited number of migratory bird species, such as waders, that come here in summer to feed, but quickly dash southwards as soon as the rearing of their young is complete.

Enquiry

Visit the PACE project website, at

http://www.cf.ac.uk/earth/pace/

1 What is the PACE project?

2 Where are their field sites in Europe?

3 Where is their field site in the UK, and what is it monitoring?

4 How does this field site compare with those in the Alps?

5 Find Svalbard and the description of the Janssonhaugen region. What processes are at work there and what features have been produced?

Living in cold environments

Cold environments represent the margins of the inhabited Earth. They are associated with isolation, but they are not without resources and development potential. Despite the challenges posed by the physical environment, resources such as fish, animals, minerals (gold, iron and uranium) and energy (coal, oil and gas) have been and still are being exploited. Recent advances in technology, together with ever rising global demands, now promise to make further exploitation highly likely, as well as rather more economic. That assumes, of course, that everyone is agreed that the cold environments should become more developed and settled. However, there is a growing body of opinion ('Green' and conservation-minded) that argues, with increasing forcefulness and passion, that large areas of the cold environments should be protected and kept in their natural state as wilderness areas.

Whilst long-established activities such as herding, fishing and forestry remain important in some cold environments, they are being increasingly challenged by modern industries such as energy development and tourism. Transport infrastructures have been expanded to facilitate these new developments, but not without adverse impacts on the natural environment. In general, we may say that the human presence and human pressure decrease across the cold environments in a polewards direction (see **1.3** on page 6). But that is not to imply that the ice environments around the poles themselves are free from trouble – far from it!

Figure 6.1 The resources of the cold environments – use, impact and challenges

Resource				
Natural pasture	Wildlife	Fish	Minerals and energy	Wilderness
Exploiting activities Nomadic herding	Hunting, tourism	Fishing	Mining, smelting, oil industry	Tourism
Environmental impact Little or none	Species depletion, disturbance	Overfishing	Air pollution, water pollution, visual pollution	Litter and garbage, visual pollution, noise pollution
Challenge To preserve the traditional way of life in a modern context	To maintain biodiversity	To conserve fish stocks	To reduce all forms of pollution to acceptable levels	To minimise the tourist footprint

Let us now look systematically at the portfolio of human activities in cold environments. Figure **6.1** summarises the situation in terms of the resources, their associated activities and their environmental impacts and challenges. Given that only a relatively small percentage of the cold environments exist in the Southern Hemisphere (mainly Antarctica), much of the discussion below will focus on the Arctic. Furthermore, given the shortage of information about developments in the Arctic regions of what was until a decade ago the Soviet Union, the focus will be sharpened still further to Alaska, Arctic Canada, Greenland and Arctic Scandinavia.

SECTION A

Updated traditional activities

Herding and hunting

The herding of reindeer by nomadic people such as the Inuits in North America and Greenland and the Sami in Lapland Europe is probably, along with hunting and fishing, the oldest economic activity of the cold environments. To use the term 'economic' may well be overstating the situation rather, because this early nomadic herding was largely about subsistence and self-sufficiency. The resource underlying this way of life was the grazing provided by the tundra during the short summer and the taiga during the long winter. It was this seasonal pattern of food availability that prompted the seasonal migrations of caribou and reindeer that persist to this day. The Inuits and Sami simply developed a survival strategy that involved following this mobile food supply. The hunting also extended to seals and bears, not just for their meat but also their fur.

The beauty of this nomadic way of life is that it is fairly well in tune with the natural environment. It is sustainable. Human impacts on the natural environment and wildlife are minimal. Whilst this way of life survives to

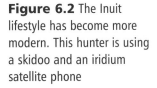

Figure 6.2 The Inuit lifestyle has become more modern. This hunter is using a skidoo and an iridium satellite phone

this day, there are signs that it has moved with the times. For example, animal-drawn sledges have been replaced by motorised skidoos (**6.2**); the herders occupy seasonal cabins rather than igloos and hide tents; and they have developed additional sources of income, such as trading in skins and furs and, more recently, selling traditional artefacts to tourists. However, the indigenous peoples of the Arctic and their lifestyle are threatened in a variety of ways:

- Their freedom to roam is being impeded by political boundaries.
- The enclosure of huge areas of the taiga for private forestry is causing a serious loss of much-needed winter grazing.
- Their rights to hunt and trade in skins are being taken away by conservation-minded legislation; this is causing a serious loss of income.
- The pollution of natural pasture by radioactive fallout from nuclear testing and other military activities is causing radionuclides to enter the human food chain, via first mosses and lichens and then via the herded livestock that feed on these plants.
- There is government pressure in the form of money and other incentives to make the herders become more sedentary. Many find that they simply cannot make the necessary adjustment and this is leading to all sorts of social problems, particularly alcoholism, drug abuse and crime.

Fishing

Although fishing was part of the traditional Arctic way of life, it has made the transition from a subsistence to a commercial activity. Indeed, it has become a major economic activity. For example, it accounts for 70 per cent of Iceland's GNP. It is the plankton richness of the high-latitude oceans that makes them so attractive to commercial fishing, for these waters are able to support huge shoals of fish. More than that, the shoals are frequently dominated by single species. This means that **by-catches** (unwanted species) are minimised. However, it also means that over-fishing is even more likely. The collapse of the herring fishery in the 1970s served as one warning, and the later exhaustion of capelin stocks another. But when over-fishing occurs and stocks diminish, it is not only the fishing industry and its employees that suffer. There are serious consequences for seabirds and cetaceans (whales and dolphins) that also rely on those stocks for survival. The case study on page 87 will also make the important point that it is not only over-fishing that threatens the livelihoods of fishermen.

Historically, Arctic freshwater resources have been of an extremely high standard. They have been renowned for their salmon and trout. However, today other activities such as forestry and mining are having a serious impact on water quality. Amongst the worst affected areas is the Kola Peninsula in Russia, where the mining and smelting of copper and nickel have led to high levels of river pollution. Fish stocks have plummeted.

Figure 6.3 These seabirds are just some of the species that rely on richly stocked Arctic seas for survival

Farming

In recent years, attempts have been made to develop more conventional modes of farming. Despite the severe restrictions imposed by the climate and the resulting shortening of the growing season to less than 90 days, there is now something in the order of 1 million ha of arable land in Alaska and Arctic Canada. This land is used primarily for the production of winter feed and silage, which are used to support the more sedentary mode of livestock-rearing. However, other crops are grown, most notably vegetables. They are grown for local consumption. They are part of what is referred to as **outpost agriculture**, aimed at growing as much as possible locally for the people of these remote regions. The range of products also includes milk, meat and eggs. The farming is hardly economic, and commodity prices are scarcely competitive compared with those of food produced much further south and transported over long distances and at considerable cost.

Forestry

It is mainly within the periglacial environments that the tundra gives way southwards to what is known as the **taiga**, with its cold temperate climate – a biome dominated by coniferous trees. But the transition zone is a broad one. Where periglacial rather than cold temperate conditions prevail, the taiga is represented by only scattered patches of forest, located in valleys and other sheltered areas. Here, one typically finds a mosaic where the stands of trees are admixed with lakes, bogs, marshes and moorland. Nonetheless, those scattered patches of forest have been exploited over the centuries as sources of construction timber and fuel. With the relentless rise in the demand for timber and pulp for paper, increasing commercial pressure has been placed on the more marginal forests. Clear-felling has led to enormous ecological disruption and the loss of biodiversity with respect to both plants and animals. On top of all this, there has been the adverse impact of acid rain generated by the burning of fossil fuels in smelters and in power stations.

Review

1 Do you think that a more sedentary livestock-herding is any less sustainable than nomadic herding?

2 Do you think that indigenous peoples should be allowed to continue their traditional hunting activities? Give your reasons.

3 What do you think are the advantages of promoting outpost agriculture rather than relying almost entirely on imported food supplies?

4 Why is commercial forestry turning to the more marginal forests?

Mineral and energy exploitation

The Arctic regions contain a range of mineral and energy resources. Perhaps the world first became aware of this endowment in the gold rushes of the 19th century, to places such as the Klondike and Nome. Since then, attention has turned to the more mundane but no less needed deposits of iron, nickel and even uranium. It has to be said that the working of these minerals has inflicted enormous and largely unpublicised environmental damage. The destruction of natural habitats, the profound disturbance of wildlife and traditional ways of life, as well as the pollution of air and water figure amongst the worst injuries. During the second half of the 20th century, however, an energy-hungry world became increasingly interested in the growing proven reserves of oil and natural gas found in the Arctic sectors of both North America and Russia. Exploitation of these is now well under way, but again not without adverse impacts on the environment. Oil spills are an obvious example, so too the construction of oil pipelines.

Case study: The pipeline problem

A major problem associated with exploiting rich oil reserves in Alaska and Arctic Canada is that of transporting the crude oil from the wells to where it is either refined or shipped for refining. The only way to do this is by pipeline. The difficulty is that in the low temperatures that prevail here, oil loses its ability to flow. It therefore has to be heated before it can be pumped. Pipes have to be:

Figure 6.4 Visual pollution – The Trans-Alaska Pipeline

- of sufficient bore (up to 12 m in diameter) to facilitate flow
- lagged to prevent heat loss
- heated to keep the oil at the optimum flow temperature.

Bearing in mind that pipelines have to constructed across vast tracts of permafrost, the problem becomes immediately obvious: How can the crude oil be kept warm and flowing without melting the permafrost? Burying the pipeline in an insulated trench is one possible solution, but it has proved difficult and very expensive to achieve the very high degree of insulation required. Suspending the pipeline above the ground on trestles is another and more widely used solution. However, it is far from perfect:

- the great weight of the lagged pipe often leads to sinking, which in turn can cause fracturing and oil spills
- the pipelines create an eyesore scar across vast tracts of land
- they have a barrier effect on migrating animals.

Case study: The *Exxon Valdez* disaster

In 1989 a supertanker, laden with 1.2 million barrels of crude oil, ran aground in Prince William Sound (Alaska). The ship, which was being piloted illegally, had just left Valdez, the terminal at the southern end of the Alaska oil pipeline. Over a quarter of a million barrels of oil leaked out during the 10 hours it took to set up the first oil containment booms and before oil-removing equipment reached the scene of the accident. The oil spread over some 25 000 km² of coastal and offshore waters.

By a year later, 35 000 dead seabirds had been found, and these were believed to represent only a small proportion of the total killed. Some 10 000 sea otters, 16 whales and 147 bald eagles were among the larger

Figure 6.5 Trying to reduce the scale of the disaster: the clean-up operation begins after the *Exxon Valdez* runs aground

animals and birds killed by the spillage. Salmon, black cod and herring spawning grounds were also decimated. Wildlife will continue to suffer the effects well into the present century.

The massive clean-up cost is believed to have cost the company that owned the supertanker over $2 billion. On top of this, in 1993, a US federal judge fined the company a record $5 billion in punitive damages. This money was used mainly to compensate 34 000 fishermen whose livelihoods had been seriously damaged by the oil spill.

Public concern aroused by the accident prompted a reconsideration of the whole issue of oil and gas exploitation in sensitive environments, particularly the wilderness areas of the Arctic. For a while, there was something of a pause in production, but today output proceeds at increasing levels. The best hope is that safeguards have been put in place that will prevent a repetition of the disaster.

Review

5 How and why is it that mining causes river pollution?

6 Identify the problems associated with the exploitation Arctic oil.

Settlement and transport

About 3.5 million people live in the Arctic. The Inuits and Lapps have lived there for some 5000 years, while non-indigenous peoples began colonising the area from about AD 1500, largely as a result of the search for new resources, markets and connecting shipping routes. Arkhangelsk, for example, was founded in 1584. The recently renewed interest in the Arctic has attracted a fair volume of in-migration. Even so, indigenous peoples still account for 80 per cent of Greenland's population, 15 per cent of Norway's and 4 per cent of Russia's. Despite the population influx, though, the cold environments of the Northern Hemisphere remain sparsely populated, with large distances and limited transport links between settlements. Settlements vary from large mining and industrial centres, such as Murmansk (400 000) and Novilisk (185 000) in Russia, to isolated farms and nomadic groups.

Case study: Keeping people, keeping Svalbard

Svalbard (formerly known as Spitzbergen) is a large island in the Arctic, governed by Norway. Although Svalbard offers few resources, Norway is keen to maintain its sovereignty over the island rather than letting it fall into the hands of rival claimants which, over the years, have included Russia, Germany, the Netherlands and even the UK. To do this requires maintaining a permanent presence on the island. For a long time, it was whaling and sealing that provided the necessary means of livelihood. However, global conservation conventions have caused such activities virtually to cease.

There are rich coal deposits and at one time there were seven mines in operation. Today, there is only one and this is kept open only for political reasons and to supply the power station that provides the main settlement, Longyearbyen (population 1100), with its electricity supply. It seems particularly ludicrous to keep this coal mine open: Norway is a country richly endowed with oil and natural gas, and it produces large amounts of hydro-electric power.

It was immediately after the First World War (1914–1918) that Norway acquired sovereignty over Svalbard. The treaty that brought this about also stipulated that any nation signing up to the agreement and recognising Svalbard as Norwegian territory had the right to mine and conduct scientific experiments there. Up until quite recently, most of the 39 nations that signed the treaty have taken advantage of these rights. During the Second World War (1939–1945) and in the Cold War era (1950–1990), Svalbard was used as an important spying post by all sides.

Figure 6.6 A cruise ship carries tourists up an iceberg-filled fjord in Svalbard

In the past two decades, Longyearbyen has become quite a popular port-of-call for cruise ships, and the younger set come to the island to snowmobile, ski or trek across the wilderness. However, the season is so short that tourism cannot really provide much support for year-round settlement. In 1993, another possible way of maintaining that settlement was launched. The Norwegian government designated Svalbard an environmental research station, and four Norwegian universities established a new campus there for 300 staff and students. The campus has since been joined by 20 scientific stations set up by foreign governments, taking advantage of the terms of the treaty that gave Norway sovereignty over 80 years ago.

Although some of these research bases will keep a few people on Svalbard all the year round, the overall population of the island will still plummet in winter. Without the one remaining coal mine, which has to be kept open all year to make it viable, the island would be completely deserted in winter.

Buildings and utilities

The most important aspect in constructing buildings, as with other structures in permafrost, is to build on coarse and well-drained material if possible. One of the problems of towns in the far north is that they are located at river mouths, river junctions or on low-lying islands, where the soil is composed largely of silt. Hence frost heave and permafrost degradation are major problems. In order to keep the permafrost intact temperature-wise, most buildings are raised up on piles sunk deep into the ground (6.7). Gravel pads and insulation are a much used solution to keeping the permafrost intact, be it in the construction of oil tanks or heavy industrial plant.

Sources of freshwater are limited in periglacial areas. In general, only the larger lakes provide adequate water storage and supply for a community of more than a few people. Water below the permafrost can be pumped up, but this is costly. Deep wells have to be sunk and those wells have to be insulated and heated to prevent freezing up. The disposal of sewage is another problem area. There are relatively few places in the Arctic that have modern sewerage systems. In the discontinuous zone, where permafrost is lacking, cesspits and septic tanks are used. In contrast, in the continuous zone, individual buckets are often literally carried and dumped in a designated spot, usually a river or lake. However, even this is a problem in the prevailing low temperatures. Where there are sewerage systems, the main problem – as with water and oil – is to keep material that is moving along pipes from freezing. Sewers cannot be placed underground without special protection and insulation. The preferred solution is to build insulated and heated pipes above the ground, encased in what are termed **utilidors** (6.7).

(a) Pile foundations for houses and wooden buildings

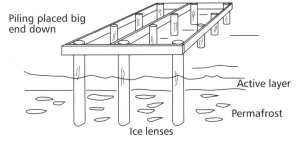

Piling placed big end down

Active layer

Permafrost

Ice lenses

(b) Thick gravel pads needed for aircraft runways

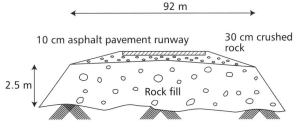

92 m

10 cm asphalt pavement runway

30 cm crushed rock

2.5 m

Rock fill

(c) The high-tech 'utilidor' system for domestic services

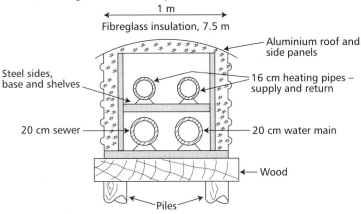

1 m

Fibreglass insulation, 7.5 m

Aluminium roof and side panels

Steel sides, base and shelves

16 cm heating pipes – supply and return

20 cm sewer

20 cm water main

Wood

Piles

(d) Gravel pad insulation and special cooling measures for oil storage

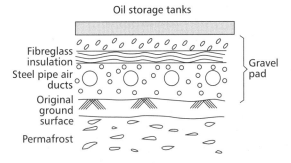

Oil storage tanks

Fibreglass insulation

Steel pipe air ducts

Original ground surface

Permafrost

Gravel pad

(e) Gravel pad insulation and special cooling measures for heavy industrial plant

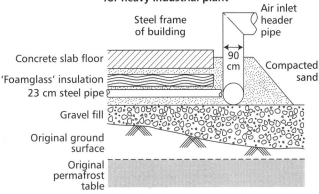

Steel frame of building

Air inlet header pipe

Concrete slab floor

'Foamglass' insulation

23 cm steel pipe

Gravel fill

Original ground surface

Original permafrost table

90 cm

Compacted sand

Figure 6.7 Coping with permafrost

Transport

Even driving a vehicle can easily become a problem in the cold environments. For example, diesel is unreliable at low temperatures, rubber loses its ability to grip, oils cease to lubricate, metals become brittle and engines are difficult to start.

There are also many problems related to road construction. For example, there are huge distances to cover and a wide range of topography to be crossed. The Alaska Highway was built in 1942–3 between Dawson Creek and Fairbanks and is over 3000 km long. Beyond Whitehorse, a quarter of

7 With reference to
  6.7, explain why
  'special cooling
  measures' are
  needed.

8 Explain why the
  permafrost presents
  an obstacle to
  settlement and
  transport.

9 Identify the main
  problems associated
  with water supply
  and sewage disposal.

the road is built on permafrost. The most effective way of insulating the permafrost and keeping it frozen has been to pile a thick layer of brushwood on to the peat moss and then to cover this with a layer of gravel. It is on the top of this gravel that the normal stages of road construction are laid. The maintenance of the roads is also something of a headache. Frost action tends to break up the surface; sporadic melting of the underlying permafrost causes sinking and slumping; and bridges are frequently destroyed by the spring meltwater floods.

Air transport is one way of overcoming the wide open spaces of the cold environments. Here too there are many obstacles, from the construction of airstrips that are not too deformed by frost and freeze–thaw processes (**6.7**) to keeping those runways clear of winter snow, and keeping aircraft free of ice and snow whilst they are on the ground.

In Alaska, many small aircraft take advantage of the many lakes and coastal inlets. For summer landings, floats are fitted, while in the winter skis are attached for landing on the ice.

SECTION D

Tourism

Tourism is fast becoming a major economic activity in the Arctic. By the early 1990s there were over 1 million visitors each year (**6.8**). The Arctic has always been perceived as a remote, unreachable and fearful part of the globe, but a combination of factors is currently responsible for boosting visitor numbers:

- the various attractions of its wilderness regions – scenery, wildlife and so on
- improved accessibility
- better infrastructure
- increased personal affluence and leisure time
- the whetting of the travel appetite by TV programmes
- the relentless search for 'new' tourist destinations and experiences.

Governments quite rightly see the potential for tourism and the possible knock-on benefits of the industry in terms of triggering development on a rather broader front. This would include:

- encouraging the growth of 'support' activities
- attracting in new settlers
- reaching population thresholds that would justify the provision of more and better services.

But, of course, there is the constant tension between the demands of the tourist industry and the environment that the tourists have come to experience. So easily, the growth of the former can bring about the decline and destruction of the latter. There is a perilous tightrope to be walked.

Figure 6.8 Tourism in the Arctic (2000)

Region	Number of tourists
Arctic Alaska	25 000
Yukon (Canada)	177 000
NW Territories (Canada)	48 000
Greenland	6 000
Iceland	129 000
Northern Scandinavia	500 000
Svalbard	35 000
Arctic Russia	No data

Case study: Tourism in Greenland

Greenland, as well as other Arctic regions, is planning to expand tourism development. The real beginning of the tourism industry here dates back to 1959, when charter flights became available to Narsarsuaq in the south and to Kulusuk in the east, where there were American bases with landing strips. Today, the tourists who come to Kulusuk, for example, are day-trippers from Iceland. They stay for about an hour – just enough time to walk around the settlement and buy some souvenirs. There are just 300 inhabitants and 3500 tourists each summer.

In 1990, the Greenland Parliament approved a plan to guide the development of the tourist industry to as far as 2005. The plan identified the key resources and attractions, and set a target of between 30 000 and 35 000 visitors a year. The motivation for the development plan was the need to find a replacement for Greenland's declining fishing industry, then the largest employer and major economic activity.

At that time, the tourism industry in Greenland was small, involving no more than a few thousand visitors a year and providing little more than 150 jobs for a total population of 55 000. So a vital part of the plan was to increase that number of jobs to between 2500 and 3000.

Factors encouraging the subsequent expansion of the industry have included:

- the pristine nature of the polar environment, with its spectacular scenery and remoteness
- the intrinsic interest of the indigenous Inuit culture.

Figure 6.9 Tourists visiting the Equi Glacier in the Disko Bay, West Greenland

At the same time, however, there have been a number of negative aspects that have hindered growth:

- the inadequate transport links, both within the country and with the outside world
- the shortness of the season during which the weather is suitable for outdoor tourism
- an inadequate hotel infrastructure
- the popular perception that there is really only one polar destination – Antarctica.

Today, despite the best efforts of the Greenland government, tourism remains an industry that is in its infancy, and a rather alien one to the inhabitants of the country. There are inherent problems. For example, it is not proving easy to train the Inuit people and make them aware of the needs and benefits of the industry. Key positions are currently occupied by Danes. Unfortunately, tourism is only possible during the short summer season, and in these months there are work opportunities in other economic activities, such as fishing and mineral exploration. Nonetheless, the case has been well made that tourism could make a much greater contribution to Greenland's economy.

Review

10 Which of the current obstacles to tourism development in Greenland do you think is the most serious? Give your reasons.

Managing polar areas

All but the last of the activities considered in this chapter currently take place mainly, but not exclusively, within the proglacial and periglacial environments. However, of all the cold environments, it is protection of the ice-covered regions around the poles that should perhaps concern us most. They are pristine; they have resources. They are also essentially uninhabited, so who is there to care if those resources are exploited and the environment happens to be damaged in the process? For most countries and many people, the fate of the polar regions is not high on the agenda. Certainly, there does not seem to be the same level of global concern about those regions as there is, for example, about the clearance of tropical rainforest and rising carbon dioxide emissions.

In terms of ensuring the future well-being of Antarctica, a landmark first step was taken with the signing of the Antarctic Treaty in 1958. The Antarctic is unusual in that it is, to all intents and purposes, uninhabited and it does not belong to any nation. It forms part of the **global commons**. Its land and resources are not legally owned, but are deemed to be the heritage of all humanity. Over the years, some nations have made political claims to territory in Antarctica. Semi-permanent scientific research stations were first established on the continent during the International Geophysical Year (1957–1958). This is the only form of settlement currently permitted (**6.10**).

Figure 6.10 The dome of the Amundsen–Scott South Pole research station, Antarctica

The Antarctic Treaty (which came into effect in 1959) put a halt to all territorial claims and created the opportunities for nations to undertake scientific research and observation. Today, 44 countries have signed up to the Treaty and many of them now have research establishments. They range from Argentina and Australia to the UK and the Ukraine. What that research has already shown is that the continent has considerable economic potential in the form of stocks of coal, iron ore and oil. Global concern about the environmental impact of any such mining or oil exploration is currently preventing any of those resources from being exploited. In the late 1980s, several nations, led by Australia and France, pressed for Antarctica to be made into a 'world park', in which there would be no mineral exploitation. However, the present moratorium on

mineral working (the Madrid Protocol of 1991) is a relatively short one and runs out in 2041. So, effectively, the threat still hangs over the continent. In the meantime, nations such as Japan and the USA continue to explore for oil.

Further and tighter legislation is also required to manage Antarctica's stocks of fish. Fleets from Russia, Japan, Taiwan, Poland and Germany are fishing extensively in Antarctic waters – mainly for krill, which is used for fertilizer and animal feed. The problem here is that krill (tiny sea creatures) are the base of the food chain that currently supports a huge amount of wildlife, particularly seabirds and cetaceans.

Finally, reference needs to be made once again to the rise of tourism in the polar regions, particularly in Antarctica. The number of tourists visiting the coasts of the continent by cruise ship rose from under 5000 in 1990 to nearly 15 000 in 2000. Although these tourists set foot on the continent only for a few hours at a time, there is growing concern about their impact on the fragile environment and its abundant wildlife. At present, it is also possible for tourists, under tight supervision, to camp on the continent, but many worry that this will soon lead to calls for the building of hotels.

At present, there are a number of controls in place aimed at ensuring that the impacts of tourism are minimised. Most cruises include on-board lectures by experts on all aspects of the continent, including codes of conduct and protocols. All the major tour operators are members of the International Association of Antarctic Tour Operators. This is a self-regulating body that lays down guidelines from the disposal of waste to the number of tourists landing at particular sites.

By comparison, the Arctic perhaps lacks some of the Antarctic's 'glamour' and the basic circumstances are rather different. For example, most of the land is owned; and it is populated. Resource exploitation has been going on for some time and with relatively little concern for environmental impacts. But it too is a wilderness region which, as we have seen, attracts a growing number of tourists. Two notable developments during the 1990s were as follows:

- The setting up, in 1991, of the Arctic Monitoring and Assessment Programme to keep an eye on pollution throughout the region.
- The signing, in 1997, of the Arctic Environmental Protection Strategy by eight Arctic countries. This encourages international co-operation in scientific research into the causes and consequences of pollution in the cold environments of the Northern Hemisphere.

At least that is a start, but there is much more to be done if large tracts of the Arctic are to be conserved for the benefit of future generations.

A final thought concerns the threat of global warming. Not only might this be expected to reduce the extent of global ice, but in so doing it will allow the other cold environment zones to extend, or perhaps retreat polewards (**1.3**). What is much less clear is the degree to which that warming might

11 Do you think that tourism in the cold environments is something to be encouraged? Give your reasons.

12 Besides checking environmental pollution, what else needs to be done to ensure that the polar wildernesses remain intact?

change the essential character of those environments, and therefore the opportunities and challenges that they currently present to people.

To sum up, the bottom line in this discussion about human use of the cold environments is really one of values. What value do we place on these environments, on these often empty, bleak and daunting places? They are places that are basically hostile to people; places that require all manner of obstacles to be overcome if they are to be 'opened up' and developed. Do we think that their landscapes and ecosystems are worth protecting and conserving as things to be enjoyed today, and hopefully tomorrow, in a leisure context by a privileged minority of affluent people? Or do we think that since Nature has endowed these environments with resources, we should not feel inhibited about using the best of modern technology to exploit them for the benefit of the majority? Where do you stand on this issue?

Enquiry

1 Read this chapter again and, with the aid of websites and other published material, put together a set of arguments to support your view on the issue 'Cold environments – conserve or exploit?'

2 Research the gold rushes to the Klondike and Nome. What were environmental conditions like for the gold prospectors? What impact did they have on the environment?

3 Write a brief report comparing Antarctica and Greenland in terms of their potential as tourist destinations.

4 Research the sorts of impact that global warming is likely to have on the three cold environments (see **1.3**).

Further reading and resources

Books and other printed publications on cold environments include the following:

Kenneth Addison, *Classic Glacial Landforms of Snowdonia* (Geographical Association, 1997)
Arctic Experience, *Key to Iceland* (Icelandic Publishing House, 1996)
Ray Bradley and Norman Law, *Climate Change and Society* (Nelson Thornes, 2001)
N. and R. Foskett, Glaciation, glacial processes and people: a case study of Iceland, *Geofile* 192 (Mary Glasgow Publications/Nelson Thornes)
Global Environmental Outlook, 2000 (Earthscan, 1999)

Here is a selection of useful websites:

http://arcticcircle.uconn.edu – the Arctic Circle website covers natural resources, history and culture and resource use, and features both a discussion forum for visitors to the Arctic Circle and a virtual classroom.

http://nsidc.org/index.html – the home page of the US National Snow and Ice Data Center.

http://nsidc.org/glaciers/ – the NSIDC's 'All About Glaciers' web page gives details of glacier research, projects and glaciological organisations online; general information and news stories concerning glaciers; and a quick tour through the life of a glacier.

http://usarc.usgs.gov – the website of the United States Antarctic Resource Center.

http://www.aad.gov.au – Antarctica Online, the website of the Australian Antarctic Division, features 'Classroom Antarctica' (http://classroomantarctica.aad.gov.au), a selection of online resources for both teachers and pupils.

http://www.antarctica.ac.uk – the website of the British Antarctic Survey provides a wealth of information about Antarctica and the Southern Ocean, including reports about the ozone hole, climate change, the ice sheet and exploitation of Antarctica.

http://www.arctic-experience.co.uk – Arctic Experience offers a range of holidays to Iceland, Greenland, Spitzbergen, Lapland and the Faroe Islands, and escorted tours in Iceland. The website features a range of information about the Arctic, including an interesting section on Arctic wildlife.

http://www.cf.ac.uk/earth/pace/ – the PACE project website provides up-to-date information on permafrost and climate change in Europe.